The Teacher's Manifesto

The Teacher's Manifesto

A Cry of Justice for All

Krishna Madan

ISBN: 1522983481
ISBN 13: 9781522983484

To
Rigoberto Ruelas Jr.,
first fatality
of
21st Century Witch Hunts.

Acknowledgements

THANK YOU, PAULA Kirifides, for your conscientious reading, corrections, and insightful comments. We miss you at school! Ευχαριστώ πάρα πολύ.

Gracias, María do los Ángeles, por su ayuda, apoyo y consejo. Recuerdo su corazón de ángel, Mari.

Mahalo, Devin and Sasha, for your encouragement and suggestions. Continue this tradition!

Thanks also to Angela Peterson, Michelle, Anthony, Kathy, Hank, Jeff F., Jeff S., Whitney, Ellen, Bryan, Patanjali, and Jorg for support and important feedback.

Finally, thanks to all of my students, past and present, for reminding me of reality every day. It will soon be your turn to change it!

Contents

Send not to know for whom the bell tolls;
It tolls for thee.

John Donne

CHAPTER 1

— ✏ —

Chaos: Kafka, Trump, and Offshore Banks

IT IS EARLY April of 2015. I am teaching World History to my 10th grade class. One of the girls, "Sue," requests permission to go to the bathroom. I ask her to wait for the return of another girl, "Mary," who left for the restroom a few minutes ago.

Sue waits patiently, fidgeting in her seat. After ten minutes, she asks again, agitatedly. I write her a pass, asking her to check up on Mary, who has been gone fifteen minutes by now.

When Sue returns, she is breathless. When queried as to why she herself is late, she announces that she heard moaning from the adjoining bathroom stall. She excitedly relates that she reached overhead in that stall with her cellphone and snapped a picture.

Sue then breathlessly continues that she immediately ran to the administration offices to show the picture to an Assistant Principal. On the cellphone, Sue relates, was a picture of Mary performing *fellatio* on a male student. Sue, of course, doesn't put it quite that delicately.

I try to hush the rest of the story. I breathe a sigh of relief that Sue shows her phone to no one. One is always grateful for small miracles in a school located in a struggling neighborhood.

We didn't see Mary again for a couple of weeks, until after her suspension was over. Even though the type of suspension Mary received allowed for alternative instruction during her absence, I doubt that her mind was quite focused on her schoolwork at that time—or for the remaining month of the school year.

Nevertheless, Mary took her various "high-stakes" tests that Florida requires on her return. These online exams themselves were plagued with numerous and repeated breakdowns and gross irregularities. Many students across the state of Florida simply stopped trying to answer questions out of sheer frustration with the entire online process.

The outraged professionals administering the exams could not believe what they were hearing from students. They could not understand what they were seeing for themselves on the computers as they desperately tried to help students. But it was all to no avail!

Programs crashed, questions recycled themselves, tests would not accept answers, and so on. Frustrated themselves, the test proctors attributed the problems to the negligence and incompetence of the private contractor that developed and administered the exams.

The costly contract that resulted in this testing chaos actually took scarce money away from teaching itself. These examiners would even get to test us again the following year, draining more funds from the counseling support that Mary desperately needs.

Moreover, it is hard to get Mary and my other students to learn much when they end up missing weeks of instruction due to the intimidating battery of exams that Florida imposes on its students. This interruption of learning is then made worse by students having to repeat defective tests.

Despite the problems in Mary's personal life and the laughable launch of this new test, Mary's scores helped to determine my pay for the current school year as well as that of my principal. The State of Florida dutifully anointed the exam results issued by the profit-making company awarded the expensive contract.

It was, in the words of one incredulous school official, as if those who observed the test chaos were just imagining things and the repeated and gross breakdowns simply didn't happen. Somehow the much-vaunted "accountability" doesn't apply at this higher level of educational policy and contracting. Instead, in many of its dealing with private contractors, the State of Florida acts like Mary in the bathroom stall.

Despite making a bad choice on that day in April 2015, Mary is actually a decent girl and a good student. She has learned from her mistake. Unfortunately, the same cannot be said of the state of Florida. Nor can it be said of the numerous other states across the country pursuing "education reform" as a pretext to reward private companies.

Welcome to education in America in the 21st Century! Kafka, who wrote about the bizarre absurdities suddenly facing a worker, would instantly recognize the incomprehensible environment in which teachers find themselves today. Unfortunately, as Kafka knew, bizarreness is a symptom of a system in deep trouble.

⅋

A specter is haunting America—the danger of educational collapse. Unlike the fictional *Specters* that supposedly plagued Salem, Massachusetts in 1692, this menace is no mere illusion. It is rather the imminent consequence of the protracted siege of budget cuts on public education culminating in the current direct attack using testing as a battering ram.

Like many real wars, this crusade against public education is motivated by blind ideology and rank greed. Those on the warpath against teachers are an unholy alliance of sexist talking heads, conservative ideologues, politically correct liberals, religious fanatics, and educational profiteers.

In a country that has long searched for scapegoats—recall the Salem witch trials, the Red Scare, and McCarthyism—educational Puritans have now whipped up witless, rabid media and legislative lynch mobs that blame teachers for the ills of education and society. Their fanatical "reforms," as is generally true with exorcism, threaten to destroy the very being the "reformers" are supposedly trying to improve—in this case, American education.

Teachers themselves have been negligent by only *reacting* to this threat, doing so *piecemeal*, and *failing to make connections* to related issues in America and around the world. Now is thus the time to look at the scapegoating of teachers from a broader societal and historical perspective. It is also the time to compare the mistreatment of mostly female teachers with the toleration of mostly male police officers when the latter perform poorly or misbehave.

Now is the time to coherently *expose the economic and political philosophy behind educational "reform"* and to show how this philosophy causes problems for others in the world and for the planet itself. The poisoning of the people of Flint is only one more outrageous example from an innumerable list of such unbelievable abuses.

The Teacher's Manifesto thus shows how the demonization of teachers results from a perfect storm of ***five virulent tendencies converging***:

1. ***Sexism***—manifest in contempt for a mostly female, feminine-type profession.
2. ***Puritan Fanaticism***—manifest in scapegoating those who are vulnerable and in promoting religious schools and religious-influenced charters at the expense of secular public schools.
3. ***Capitalist Opportunism***—manifest in targeting for privatization those vulnerable schools in failing

communities betrayed by our economic system and our politicians.

4. *Neoliberal Ideology*—manifest in the proclamation of catchy free-market slogans that sound attractive but which disappoint when privatization is actually implemented.

5. *Liberal Betrayal*—manifest in failing to get to the root of the problems facing poor and minority youth and in savagely blaming teachers instead.

Teachers, professionals, and workers around the world all face problems that are related and derived from the injustices perpetrated by the free-market economic and political doctrine called *neoliberalism* (no connection to political liberalism). This fundamentalist ideology will be defined, explained, and thoroughly described in Chapters Four, Six, and Seven.

For now, let us just briefly look at the Flint tragedy to show what neoliberalism has wrought there and *how the issues affecting teachers are intrinsically connected to other issues of justice*:

- By attempting to privatize the water supply, the governor of Michigan—a venture capitalist—has poisoned the kids of Flint with various neurotoxins, including lead. Guess who will be blamed when the brain-damaged kids fail the standardized tests he mandates?

- A dictatorial "Emergency Manager" of Flint had earlier been appointed by the governor to replace Flint's elected city council and mayor. This unelected ruler sent forth the edict that would poison the people of the city with the water from the heavily polluted Flint River.
- The "Emergency" ruler of Flint, Darnell Earley, then wielded equivalent power in a similarly dictatorial manner in his next position—Emergency Manager of the Detroit Public Schools.
- Is it any wonder that under such neoliberal management, public school systems such as Detroit's have also been poisoned?

The bizarreness and injustice affects not only education but the whole country—and indeed, the entire world, for such is the long reach of free-market neoliberalism. The lack of international banking regulations enables wealthy corporations and individuals to bank in offshore havens like Panama. They thus dodge the taxes that would improve both schools and municipal services in revenue-starved cities like Flint. Injustice harms not only students but our very water.

We get poisoned water and decaying schools when we tolerate a political system in which the rich can buy elections. We get failing communities like Flint when we put government in the hands of those who are philosophically opposed to the very idea of governing. We basically get injustice when we turn government over to those whose only purpose is to enrich corporations rather than to build the country.

Bizarre injustice has resulted in the rise of Donald Trump. People know that the economic and political systems are rigged and are desperately looking for solutions to their economic and social dislocation. They want a strongman who would use emergency powers to implement them.

Those of us not under Trump's sway can provide a more constructive alternative for Americans. We can begin to understand the interrelated problems that affect teachers, Americans, and people around the world. We can resolve to go to the roots of those problems instead of being distracted by their symptoms.

Fighting alone, we will each continue to fight losing battles. This book is therefore not only for teachers but for *every professional, worker, and citizen* who cares about the declining working conditions and living standards with which we are all now confronted.

United in knowledge about the *full extent, history, and interconnections of the larger problems that underlie the ones in our schools*, we can not only save education but also change the future of our country and the world.

CHAPTER 2

— ℛ —

Salem Witches

For nearly a thousand years, the peoples of Western Europe and America have been periodically convulsed by a murderous fear of enemies whom they have fashioned in their own image and likeness. Jews, Muslims, heretics, Communists, and women have all at times been presented as the enemies of society. Often they were described in ways that revealed <u>a profound disturbance</u> in the Western psyche.

In Europe, the fantasies that showed Jews as child-slayers displayed an almost oedipal fear of the parent faith; the conviction that women had sex with demons and flew through the air to worship Satan in orgiastic parodies of the Mass showed a truly diabolic <u>terror of sexuality and the female</u>. Crusades and inquisitors sought out these <u>imaginary foes</u> and killed them. [i]

KAREN ARMSTRONG

WHY WERE WOMEN scapegoated in Salem? What does this have to do with the targeting of teachers today? Let us go back in time to find out...

The Salem Crucible

It is the year 1692—a time of deep malaise in rural Massachusetts. Bad weather, crop failures, and population increase have created an economic insecurity that has people on edge.

New England Puritans are worried that England will impose Anglicanism—which they consider "Popery without a Pope" —on the strict, God-fearing colony. The new English government has already decreed that the colony will have to admit immigrants of other religions, including the despised Quakers who seem to conduct themselves in church as if possessed by the Devil.

There is even physical danger. Catholic French Canada claims much of New England and periodically dispatches raiding parties, composed of French colonists and Indian tribes, to plunder Maine, New Hampshire, and New York. Refugees from the attacks flow into Massachusetts, especially Boston and Salem, raising fears that the colony could be the next target if the northern border colonies fall.

In Salem itself, the hardships of rural life in a new land enervate the psyche and raise the emotions. Neighbors are still angry at each other, a residue of the bitter struggle as to who would be the Puritan minister of the village. They still argue now about his pay. The more traditional rural farmers in inland Salem Village resent the more commercial and worldly inhabitants of coastal Salem Town who seemed to have abandoned the purity of the original faith by worshipping instead *the golden calf*—the pursuit of wealth. With time, the resentments of the simple farmers have fermented into dire suspicions.

Three generations after the first Puritans left England, the people of Salem are discovering that their home is not the New Jerusalem—God's perfect new society of pure believers—that their grandparents envisaged. Of all the stressors, this spiritual stress—the nagging sense of a God-fearing people that they have failed God—is probably the worst.

Accumulated stress from a barrage of chronic problems over the years has finally created the need for an outlet. Some children in Salem start displaying epileptic-like behavior: screaming and throwing things around—even during sermons! However, the adults need a release also. Their release will come soon—*in the way they react to the kids' problems.*

The problems of rural society in 17th century Massachusetts have created such stresses in the lives of the adults that they overreact to the problems of their children. The viscerally cruel form of their overreaction seems incomprehensible to us today but it has an explanation. It derives from a religion that provides both the impetus and ideological justification for the ensuing murderous scapegoating.

The Puritans believe in an evil force, Satan, which subverts society through the actions of weak or ill-intentioned mortals. Satan is particularly intent on destroying societies, such as their own, that are favored by God for their devoutness. Thus the bizarre behavior of Salem's children must be the result of spells cast by those in league with the Devil. The only way to protect the children is to catch those responsible for casting the spells.

In attempting to address their problems, the Puritans do not have the benefit of sociological and psychological research available to later generations. They do not know how religious problems and insecurity—whether economic, social, political, or military—can affect the behavior of individuals and groups. Not having access to the knowledge of the various social sciences that would later develop, they cannot rationally analyze their problems and devise a sensible course of action to solve or at least cope with the difficulties.

The Puritans also do not have access to analyses of scapegoating throughout history. They lack the psychological and sociological tools to critically examine themselves and stop themselves from falling into the common human trap of *finding a defenseless group to blame for problems that society finds intractable.*

From the simple perspective of the Puritans, they have come to the New World to establish a perfect, God-fearing society that is now being ruined by malevolent individuals and groups within their midst. These evil ones must therefore be punished!

Thus, a frantic search ensues to find those responsible for the maladies of the children. As usual, *women make convenient scapegoats.* Suspicion zeroes in on Tituba, a storytelling slave who regales the village girls with tales of her native Caribbean island. The stories teach the kids about another land and foreign customs. Even worse, Tituba plays games of magic with the girls.

Tituba is therefore one of the first to be arrested. Two other women are also apprehended and jailed. Arresting, incarcerating, interrogating, and accusing these three women prove so satisfying that the search for culprits expands and unconsciously morphs into a larger witch-hunt for those responsible for the ills of society.

The privations of life caused by bad weather, crop failures, population increase, and enemy attacks are seen as God's punishment for society having too long tolerated witches in its midst. The new anxiety provoked by the prospect of having to tolerate popery and heretics similarly incites a desire to root out any insidious danger where it may already exist.

Thus, authorities and townspeople now accuse and imprison numerous innocent women and some men on the charge of being witches in league with the Devil. For the good folk of Salem, the accused are treacherous fiends within their midst who have bewitched the town's children and even other adults.

Actually, some of the targeted women are those who have either challenged the well-connected and society itself or simply think and act differently. The town of Salem collectively lets out its frustration about the hardships of life in an emotional catharsis that is no less orgiastic for being Puritan in form.

As the trials approach, the accusers knowingly point to signs and the *results of tests* that indisputably amount to certifiable proof that the accused have practiced witchcraft. One such confirmation is *spectral evidence*. Many of the accusers say they have been temporarily possessed. They claim to have seen specters of their neighbors hovering around them, specters that are obviously the cause of their afflictions. Thus, the very delusions of the afflicted are considered as evidence against the accused neighbors.

Another piece of evidence is the result of the *witch cake test*. In this test, the urine of an afflicted person is mixed with rye meal, made into a cake, and then fed to a dog. If the suspected witch cries out or even gasps when the dog bites into the concoction, she is obviously guilty.

A third test is the *pin test*. In this test, needles that have been secretly dulled are used to softly probe any raised moles of the accused. If the latter does not detect the dulled needles, her supposed insensitivity to touch in the areas in question is deemed evidence of *witches' teats*—valid proof that she is a witch.

A final test is the *touch test*. In this, a suspected witch is forced to lay her hands on a supposed victim who is falling into fits. If the alleged victim then quiets down, this return to normalcy is considered proof that the suspect is indeed a witch.

These *tests*, the reasoning behind them, and the very idea of finding witches to blame will seem absurd to later generations. However, at this time, *the leading intellects are actively promoting such beliefs, practices, and tests.* Thomas Browne, a prominent English doctor and philosopher, has only been dead for ten years. He was a prolific science writer in the tradition of Francis Bacon and his support for *spectral evidence* has been used to convict women of witchcraft.

Similarly, the use of the *witch cake* in 1692 is based on the assertion of the recently deceased eminent philosopher Descartes of the existence of "effluvia." Descartes thought effluvia to be invisible particles projected outward by our bodies that enable us to see and hear the objects upon which the particles land. In Salem, Descartes' ideas are now interpreted in this manner: witches are believed to bewitch others by directing their satanic effluvia unto the bodies of their victims, saturating the latter with such secreted projections.

Thus the dog biting into the cake laced with urine from a bewitched victim would actually be gnawing into the effluvia of the culprit, causing the witch to wince as her bodily projections are attacked. This belief, note well, is based on the writings of the same Descartes (1596–1650) who is known to be one of the greatest minds in history! Although he himself did not seem to promote the *witch cake* test, his philosophical ideas are now used in 1692 to give it a rationalization that is apparently coherent.

Many of the witch tests are therefore either explicitly certified by the highest intellects or apparently compatible with their teachings. The tests are similarly sanctioned by the highest political authorities. With such authoritative support, the actual use of the tests in determining who is a witch is further buttressed by analyses by such intellects that witchcraft is indeed a serious problem in the world.

Earlier, at the turn of the 15th Century in Europe, two monks published *Witches Hammer* (original Latin title, *Malleus Maleficarum*). This was an exhaustive compendium of the various powers of witches, their numerous nefarious acts, and an analysis of the underlying cause of such evil—*the incorrigible "wickedness of women."*

Since the Pope himself approved the book and monks were among the few people who were educated, *Malleus Maleficarum*—though published almost two centuries earlier—has had the continuing effect of legitimizing and reviving a fear of witches. A new profession has developed, that of the *"witch-finder,"* who employs the various tests to rid society of witches—and earn a decent living for himself in the process.

The revived fear of witches has crossed the Atlantic and is now taking root in the new American colonies as insecurity in society provides fertile soil for its growth. (Remember both the misogynist book and the witch-hunting profession well; like other aspects of Salem, we will find them reincarnated later.)

In these new colonies, well-educated and highly influential political and religious leaders have continued the ideological campaign against witches. They publish learned treatises that have full credibility because of their authors' stations in life. One such leader, Increase Mather, writes *Remarkable Providences*. His book points to the possession of young women as just one example of numerous, unnerving devilish occurrences that are the consequences of the colonists becoming less devout.

Increase Mather's son, Cotton Mather, publishes *Memorable Providences, Relating to Witchcraft and Possessions.* This book continues the father's work by documenting the toll of witchcraft throughout the ages. These recent, local books have been widely read in New England and their stories are recounted with apprehension. These alarming accounts, and the other historical treatises on witchcraft, provide unassailable theoretical justification for those with a propensity—or motive—to accuse.

Indeed, the residents of Salem have failed to note the motivations of the accusers who lead them in the travesty of witch hunting. They are so caught up in the exhilaration of accusations and the expected satisfying vengeance against those responsible for society's misfortune that they have stopped thinking rationally.

Questions about the motives of the accusers just seem so petty— a distraction from dealing with the present danger. Thus, the good people of Salem have failed to note the manner in which the adults who lead the chorus of condemnation can *benefit materially* at the expense of those being accused.

One such motive for false accusations lies in the tension between the dual strands of medicine that exist in our colonial America. The fact that men practice one strand and women the other exacerbates the conflict. Men who practice medicine claim to be scientific and proudly call themselves doctors or physicians. The female healers quietly administer traditional folk medicine.

The male strand of medicine in colonial America considers itself modern and proper. However, in 1692, the Scientific Revolution is still in its infancy and medicine based on real science hardly exists. This is especially true in the colonies, far away as they are from the new scientific developments in Europe which are themselves only rudimentary and often speculative. On the other hand, the females use simple herbs and techniques that have proven their effectiveness over millennia. This reality is fast colliding with the male hype.

The two strands of medicine compete for patients. The male doctors disdain the traditional practices of the women in favor of the latest and supposedly more effective "scientific" techniques. Unfortunately for these sophisticated practitioners, "science" puts them at a disadvantage.

In line with the highly speculative medical ideas of notable scientists such as Bacon and Browne, one "superior" technique employed by the male doctors rests on the frequent diagnosis that the patient has "excess blood." The male medical establishment believes that excess blood causes a host of ailments. The proper treatment for this prevalent and apparently dangerous condition consists of *bleeding the patient.*

When stumped, the male doctors frequently practice their go-to remedy of bleeding, i.e., cutting the patient to let the excess blood flow out until the afflicted exhibits an amelioration of his symptoms. Many a genius doctor has ameliorated his patient to the point of actual death from believing in this cure. However, the male doctors stubbornly continue the bizarre practice. (Remember this fanatically-practiced, deadly procedure well. We will find it reincarnated in modern economics!)

It is therefore hardly a surprise that the women healers—though less dramatic—are often more effective than the male doctors. Moreover, the women even charge less! As a result, many people naturally turn to the female folk healers. This offends the professional self-respect of the male doctors who are thoroughly filled with the sense of their own importance.

In a sexist and superstitious society, success comes at a heavy price. The male doctors in our colonial America protect their pocketbooks by accusing the women healers of witchcraft. These important establishment physicians claim that their expert but failed ministrations—such as bleeding the patient—have been sabotaged by such witches. They further explain the success of women healers as due to their being in league with the Devil. Some of the Salem women now rounded up on accusations of witchcraft are indeed such folk healers. (Also remember this shifting of blame. This too will be reincarnated.)

Apart from medical competition, another motive for condemning others in Salem is that some of the accusers can benefit handsomely from the possessions of those they attack. Here again, ruthless male opportunists target women.

Earlier, in the 1630s, single women in England were promised parcels of land called "maid lots" in order to entice them to settle in the colony. This incentive has worked. In 1692, women are now more numerous than men in Massachusetts. Some still remain single. Many single women thus either continue to own such property granted as an immigration incentive or are widows who inherited property from their husbands.

On the eve of the trials in the early 1690's, the enterprises of these industrious women—whether agricultural or mercantile—now compete with those of men. In many cases, these are the type of women who find themselves accused. Not coincidentally, the accusers are often males who own adjoining property. The latter want to extend their holdings at the expense of their female neighbors whose single status makes them vulnerable to lurid speculation.

Wealthy and influential landowners like Thomas Putnam take the lead. Indeed, Putnam actually turns out to be the most prolific accuser, and Putnam's daughter, Ann, is one of the first claiming to be afflicted. She declares that she is haunted by the evil specters of certain Salem residents. Since minors cannot write out their own charges, Putnam writes out the charges for her—as he does for others, for a total of 121 times!

Interestingly enough, many of those whose specters haunt Ann just happen to be either those whom Thomas

Putnam dislikes or those on whose property he has set his eyes. Thus, political opponents of the Putnams in both Salem Town and Salem Village find themselves accused of witchcraft.

Farming residents of the village similarly find themselves under attack by this conniving family. Among the numerous innocents accused by Putnam are Rebecca Nurse and her sisters. They are influential women in the Porter family, rivals of the Putnams. Also accused is the male landowner Giles Corey—vulnerable like the single women because he is aged.

The jails of first Salem and then Massachusetts begin to fill up. In them, about 200 accused witches languish, awaiting their fate. Some of the accused die in prison. Eighteen are hanged, including Rebecca Nurse.

Outwitting those who would use the law to steal from his family, Giles Corey transfers his property to his descendants. He knows that if convicted, property that stayed in his possession would be forfeit. Corey then refuses to enter a plea, a protest against the injustice of the court and an effort not to dignify the proceedings. His refusal also stalls the trial because without a plea by the accused, the court cannot continue to try this defendant.

The clever Putnam, however, has a solution. He convinces the court—via more spectral visitations experienced by his daughter—that Corey must be forced to enter a plea by "pressing." Corey is therefore subjected to a medieval torture called *peine forte et dure* (hard and severe punishment) that has already been discontinued in England. This old man—well into his eighties—is laid flat on the ground, a board is placed on his chest, and stones are increasingly piled on the board while questions are hurled at him.

Corey will not give his tormentors the satisfaction of a response. He answers each command to make a plea by gasping, "More weight!" His breathing becomes increasingly labored until his tongue pops out of his mouth. One of the court officials pushes it back in.

Eventually, Corey's ribs crack, puncturing his lungs. Blood spurts out of his mouth as his chest caves in. Those in Salem who have retained their sanity await new developments with trepidation.

Salem as Model for America

In Salem of 1692, we see the beginning of a pattern that would be repeated continually in America. When faced with societal problems, *scapegoats* would be sought. At times, *females* would especially be targeted. Like the male doctors of Salem, politicians would *shift the blame* for their failures onto vulnerable women. *Ideology* would trump reason.

Greed would mask itself as a patriotic impulse seeking only to protect and improve the community. *Concern for the young* would be exploited. Persecution would cloak itself with a *scientific veneer.* The tormenting of the vulnerable would be justified by *tests*, their validity attested to by the *experts*. The *ambitious* would further their aims by using tests to weed out those who stand in the way of greater profits.

In the further course of American history, righteous campaigns would be directed at the "Murderous Redskin," the "Licentious Black," and the "Shiftless Mexican." These suspect populations would at times be terrorized or even ethnically cleansed by settlers, the US Cavalry, the KKK, and militias like the Texas Rangers.

The scientific and moral justification for these crusades would be found in racial pseudoscience and the supposed Biblical condemnation of outcast races. In reality, the convoluted "scientific" rationalizations and the high-sounding moral rhetoric merely masked the lust for Indian and Mexican land and the desire for cheap black labor.

In the later course of American history, as American power increased, *righteous campaigns would expand to include external as well as internal enemies.* Thus the domestic anti-communist hysteria of the 1920s was reincarnated as a worldwide anti-communist crusade of the 1950s, directed most viciously at the people of the "Third World."

As with the hapless women of Salem, the victims of witch-hunting campaigns abroad would include the rural poor. The only crime of the rural poor and the urban working class of Asia, Africa, and Latin America was to try to better their lives by demanding more responsive governments. These demands by the people of the Global South were inevitable because the capitalism of their imperial masters had not only failed them but actually debased their conditions of life.

In places like Vietnam, the Congo, and Guatemala (as reflective of Asia, Africa, and Latin America, respectively), the Puritan impulse to cleanse out the Devil and his subterfuge would therefore lead to the discovery of a threatening *Communist Menace* with its evil, atheistic bent. This was a menace that had to be destroyed to protect our way of life.

As in Salem, though, there was a deeper, unspoken motive. Just as Thomas Putnam engineered hysteria about witches to seize the land of his neighbors in 1692, so did the United Fruit Company of 1954 engineer hysteria about communists to continue to hold Guatemalan land for its profitable agribusiness. Like Salem, Guatemala was then purified—through a CIA-organized coup—of those who cast the spell of social reform over its people.

With the decline of Communism in the 1990s, a new enemy had to be found. At first, George W. Bush pointed to an "Axis of Evil." Later, he and the country settled into a *Crusade* against Islamic terrorism. Few people mentioned the embarrassing fact that Islamic fanaticism and terrorism had become a serious problem precisely because the United States itself had armed, trained, and directed Muslim jihadists in the fight against reformist socialism and communism.

The anti-communist crusade destroyed secular leftist governments and movements wherever Islam existed, thereby replacing secular society in Muslim countries with the fundamentalism and fanaticism that plague the world today. Instead of prompting self-reflection, the discovery of the new enemy of *Islamic Terrorism* merely showed the necessity for a new crusade—sending troops to lands that just happened to have oil or other resources.

But who would be the internal enemy? As with Salem in 1692, economic, military, social, and political instability would lead to the discovery of a new enemy at home. And as with Salem, those with powerfully grasping political and economic interests would lead the charge against this enemy. Once again, this enemy would be those who were vulnerable.

The America of the 21st Century thus discovered an internal enemy of *irresponsible*, *untrustworthy women*, an enemy whose evildoing was *debilitating its children*. As in Salem, this enemy could be *uncloaked through the use of tests*. And, as in Salem, this enemy would have to be *severely dealt with*.

CHAPTER 3

Barbarians on the Warpath!

America's Search for Scapegoats

IT IS THE first quarter of the twenty-first century—a time of deep anxiety in a fairly new land called America. Uncertainty and the restlessness it produces make the rapidly changing times feel like the age of the ancient apocalyptic barbarian upheavals. It is a time of societal cataclysms, mythic monsters, rabid chieftains, and ravishing barbarian queens.

It is a time when an act of the gods—the *financial* gods, that is—recently devastated the land. The *Great Market* crashed years earlier producing the *Great Recession* and untold suffering. The worth of people's dwellings plummeted and some unfortunates were being thrown out of their abodes. More and more workers were losing their jobs as merchants retrenched or even folded.

There is now palpable fear of a repeat. *Great Corrections* slam the highest marketplace regularly. Are they omens of another *Great Depression*? The unpredictability of the supreme god called *The Fed* produces great anxiety. So does the inexorably tragic Greek drama of Athens fending off the *Eurozone* behemoth. As if recalling the ancient monster Grendel, the financial seers warn that a new beast—the feared *Grexit*—will soon stalk the land.

The aged must continue to toil because the value of their hoardings has nosedived and their allowances have been cut. People have to work harder and longer for wages that are worth less because of rising prices. There is a growing realization that the next generation will not be able to enjoy the fairly decent life of their parents and grandparents. The economic insecurity has people on edge.

An unholy trinity of firearms, religion, and wars inspire dreads. Unhinged citizens shoot masses of their countrymen. People fear for their lives. The country has recently been spectacularly attacked from the air by radical Muslims from abroad. Since then, there have also been other mass killings by such fanatics. More atrocities have only been averted by the regular uncovering of plots conceived by such extremists at home.

America, formerly considering itself invincible, continually loses soldiers in interminable wars in Muslim countries. People tire of those wars and the deaths of their young. Yet the nation's leaders are also threatening new wars against several other Muslim countries that are branded as threats because they are unstable or supposedly possess horrific weapons. Our military and intelligence cadre are spread out in a host of other countries. Their purpose, we are told, is to combat fanatic Muslim terrorists.

Like malevolent *Phoenixes*, once-subdued enemies arise and seem to spread their wings aggressively. China builds a new island nest. Is it a launching pad for aerial attacks?

Russia seems to stretch her claws—in places that *we* desire. Persia sends flocks of troops abroad, gaining power at our expense.

Even democratic nations in Latin America angrily squawk at us, refusing to cooperate in our deadly crusade against hallucinatory powders and elixirs. They even make pacts with our enemies! From what our leaders tell us, there seems to be no end to the list of peoples and nations that would do us harm.

America itself is deeply divided between the "red" and the "blue" clans. Many people are still angry about a stolen election, a bitter omen that ushered in the new millennium. The most recent elections have also left much acrimony, with many believing that a foreign-born Muslim now rules the land and is determined to destroy it from within. These fearful ones smolder with resentment and hate the woman who would be the next leader just as much.

Some regional chiefs openly talk of breaking away and weapons are defiantly and even threateningly brandished in the open. An armed group has actually taken over a government camp in the West! A new political movement that viscerally opposes both the president and urbane liberals conjures up the image of a rabid, resentful populace armed with pitchforks.

Those armed with verbal pitchforks only recently directed their pointed thrusts at a powerful woman who helped to create a new form of healing opposed by the established male doctors. Like the female folk healers of Salem, this woman, Pelosi, helped those unfortunates whose ailments had been left unattended. For daring to threaten the coffers of the male doctors by ensuring medical care for all, Pelosi was called a "wicked witch."

The woman who would be our next leader is subjected to witch-hunting probes, recalling Salem's physical probes for "witches' teats." Like the witches of Salem, Hillary is condemned for machinations conducted in secret beyond the eyes of authorities. Ambitious challengers to her leadership even accuse her of being responsible for the deaths of innocent Americans abroad.

The greatest woman-hater among the chieftains vying for leadership boasts of his sexual organs and routinely insults women. He even resurrects the ancient tribal taboos against women's menstrual cycle.

The looming new contest for a leader raises the anger of citizen against citizen, with one group championing the most angry and unstable of men. Within this crazed group, a woman chieftain named sagely cautions, *"During anxious times, it can be tempting to follow the siren call of the angriest voices."* For such wisdom, she herself—like Cassandra of old—is set upon by other rabid chieftains.

The most rabid chieftain is a wild-eyed, wild-haired bully. He loudly promises to make the tribe great again and threatens rebellion if the other chieftains don't support him. Like Attila and Genghis Khan, this would-be overlord promises to unleash unrestrained violence against enemies at home and abroad. He promises to build a *Great Wall* to keep out invading hordes.

This chieftain is despised by many. However, a beautiful barbarian queen from the North is in love with him. She wants to be his mate, if not in bed at least in the tents of power. She is indeed bloodthirsty enough to be his match. In her kingdom, she has been known to kill large game with her bare hands!

From her tent in the far North, this barbarian queen has kept an eye on the menacing Russian steppes and the fearsome Slavs. With such qualifications, she is ready to share the task of leadership of the tribal confederacy in order to smite enemies at home and abroad.

Other politicians and citizens also quarrel over migrating tribes entering the land. Some welcome settlers but others see them as a threat. In some areas vigilantes attack newcomers, and politicians pass laws to restrict and expel these "illegal aliens." In other areas, citizens provide sanctuary for the besieged migrants.

Many Americans suspect that Muslim newcomers in particular are untrustworthy, call them an insidious threat, and demand them to be thrown out. Innocent Muslims are thus taunted or even attacked around the country.

The unhinged chieftain competing for power rails against Muslims and other minorities, demanding that the land be rid of *all* migrants. His tribal gatherings are orgies of anger in which people who look or think differently are viciously attacked. As the nation declines, minorities and women are under siege from this chieftain and other demagogues.

Cultural wars break out regularly. Rural citizens condemn city dwellers as unpatriotic, ungodly hedonists. Some citizens from the hinterlands condemn others from the coasts or the North, including the President himself, for losing the values of old and don't even consider them to be "real Americans."

Citizens attack and even kill each other over issues like abortion, marriage, school prayer, and teaching evolution. Tempers fray easily. In separate incidents in Florida alone, a teenager and two men have been shot for wearing a hoodie, texting during a show, and playing music disliked by the shooter.

Black men are often killed by the police. In response, African-Americans protest in the streets. Riots break out. In South Carolina, a young white teenager massacres black churchgoers. Many feel uncomfortable, and even betrayed, that a traditionally white, Christian nation has apparently suddenly become multi-ethnic, multicultural, and multi-religious. The symbol of the nation being led by a black man whose father was an African Marxist of Muslim descent is too bitter of a pill for many to swallow.

Even worse, while America falters, other nations seem to be forging ahead. Countries like India and China, which only recently were derisively mocked as "basket cases," are now overtaking America in many areas of industry. Even Brazil—once seen as an overgrown banana republic that was only good for soccer and Carnival excess—now has a booming economy that is growing much faster than America's.

Little Chile, whose economy is also booming, recently made a spectacularly precision rescue of its miners from deep below the earth's surface—a notable contrast to America's failure to rescue its own citizens from the rooftops when the hurricane hit the famed Gulf city. In education, the basis for a strong economy, American students continue to perform worse than others. The shame of being "beaten" by those we consider inferior is intolerable.

Environmental catastrophes that recall Biblical curses of pestilence and damnation increase the impending sense of doom. Like Moses turning the Pharaoh's waters red, an oil spill has recently killed much life in the Gulf and rendered it toxic. Temperatures rise and spawn steaming hurricanes that destroy the land on the coast. Heat waves, increasing in intensity each year, destroy crops and kill hundreds. From the nether regions of the frozen lands, icebergs dislodged by the warming Earth wander into sea lanes, occasionally terrorizing ships and oil rigs.

Even the heavens launch dire warning attacks. Cold storms spawned by *Polar Vortexes* ravage the land and kill hundreds while heat bolts of air pierce the desolate North, threatening to melt ice sheets and flood the land. Indeed, as a new year breaks, massive inundations swamp the heartland, as if bringing back the curse of Noah's deluge.

In its third century after declaring independence from England, America is feeling very vulnerable. The idea that America is a special country that is uniquely blessed is continuously contradicted by rapidly unfolding events that seem beyond our control.

What happened? Who has been sabotaging America? Who is to blame?

A Quiet Death: Rigoberto Ruelas, Jr.

When Gregor Samsa woke up one morning from unsettling dreams, he found himself changed in his bed into a monstrous vermin.

FRANTZ KAFKA, *THE METAMORPHOSIS*

On Sunday September 26, 2010, a fifth-grade teacher named Rigoberto Ruelas Jr. hurled himself off a bridge in Big Tujunga Canyon, California into a ravine 100 feet below. He had become severely despondent after hearing that the *Los Angeles Times* had labeled his teaching "less effective."

Why had Rigoberto been labeled "less effective?" The designation did not come from his employer, the Los Angeles Unified School District. Nor was it a summary evaluation of his performance. Rigoberto was publicly branded a "less effective" teacher *solely* because of his students' scores on standardized tests.

Rigoberto taught in an elementary school in an extremely poor neighborhood in Los Angeles dominated by gangs. For most of his students, English was a second language. The difficulties in the students' home life and the dysfunctions of their neighborhood inevitably impacted their standardized English and Math scores—just as such dysfunctions are inevitably reflected in the neighborhood's crime rate, drug use, alcoholism, and so on. Indeed, on learning of Rigoberto's death, a former student said, *"It's not his fault the students were low."* [ii]

However, whereas cops don't get the blame for the *crime statistics* in the neighborhoods they patrol, teachers get the blame for the *test statistics.* Police precincts in Los Angeles are not rated, but the schools are. The rating for Rigoberto's school was even worse than his personal one; it was deemed "least effective."

The ratings published by the *Los Angeles Times* ignored that Rigoberto was very seldom absent from school, mentored youths prone to join gangs, and ceaselessly encouraged kids to attend college. Showing his devotion to the school, he lived only a few blocks from it, and spent extra time at lunch, after school, and on weekends with students.

Rigoberto's whole life was dedicated to helping his students. Former students said that he *"took the worst students, and tried to change their lives."* [iii] Rigoberto's very purpose in life—his whole psyche—was based on his effort with his students. As someone astutely noted, in trying to change their lives, Rigoberto was risking his own. [iv]

Rigoberto's dedication mattered little to the *Los Angeles Times.* It mattered little to those who rate schools and teachers. To those Salem-like judges, the issue is simple: there are problems with American education and culprits have to be found.

Experts feverishly pored over "data" to find the malefactors. The pillars of the Los Angeles community examined the results of standardized tests—the modern equivalent of witch-test—with the medieval scrutiny of the Inquisition. Then, with somber authority, they declared Rigoberto to be a culprit. *He was a modern-day witch harming our children.*

Rigoberto thus woke up one morning and found that his life had turned into that of Gregor Samsa in Kafka's *The Metamorphosis.* He was now considered *a monstrous vermin.* Like the accused witches of Salem, Rigoberto was publicly humiliated. And like accused witches throughout the ages, he paid with his life.

CHAPTER 4

――― ✑ ―――

Teachers as Witches

Salem happened in the New World. The Protestant Reformation—of which the Puritans were the proud vanguard in the seventeenth century—claimed to have thrown aside the medieval shibboleths of Catholic Europe. The American Revolution would be fueled by the ideals of the Enlightenment, its Constitution inspired by the Age of Reason. Yet, like Europe, the United States would continue to be plagued by the primitive terrors that lie beyond the control of rationality.

It is a reminder that, however modern and scientific our society, we can still be <u>haunted by inner demons, which we project outward onto others with abhorrent effect</u>. During the twentieth century in both Europe and America, we have seen—and continue to see—some of the most savage "witch-hunts" of all time. ⱽ

KAREN ARMSTRONG

Perfection is a disease of a nation....We try to fix something, but you can't fix what you can't see. It is the soul that needs the surgery.

JULIA ROBERTS

IMAGINE YOU LISTENED to the news and heard this: *Learned Treatises about Flying Wizards and Evil Covens; Frenzied Inquisitions; Denunciations and Witch Confessions; Witch-Tests, Witch-Hunts, and Witch-Denials; Punching Witches.* You would be forgiven for imagining that the Salem of 1692 was being discussed. However, these are practically the headlines today—when the topic is teachers!

The Witches' Covens

Rigoberto Ruelas Jr. did not only kill himself because his name was published in the Los Angeles Times as a "less effective" teacher; his suicide occurred in a context where his colleagues around the nation are being attacked on all sides by the media, businessmen, conservatives, liberals, and professional politicians, including the President of the United States.

Our leaders are convinced that Rigoberto's accomplices—who are mostly female—are characterized by a baleful neglect towards the young. But they have even worse fears. These powerful authorities believe that schemers hatch malevolent plots against children in *the modern equivalent of the witches' coven—the teachers union.*

In the very same week that the harassed Rigoberto jumped into the accepting ravine and into peaceful oblivion, a film was being promoted on *Oprah* about kids waiting for a virtuous flying wizard (i.e. Superman) to rescue them from the bad witches (i.e. teachers) at schools. The promotional picture for the film shows a lone student amidst a desolation that could have only been wreaked by those engaged in sorcery.

The intent and impact of this anti-teacher film is eerily similar to that of the late medieval, misogynist *Witches' Hammer* (discussed earlier) which warned against the evils of women. In its revival of the ancient calumny that "where there is a suffering child, look for an evil woman," the film should therefore actually be renamed *Witches' <u>Chalk</u>*. It is apparently by waving sticks of such chalk that our modern witches cast their spells to stupefy our youth. This witch-hunting film is, of course, *Waiting for Superman*.

The week after Rigoberto died, multi-billionaire Bill Gates announced that his foundation would spend *half a billion dollars* to find out what constitutes effective teaching, under the gross assumption that American kids weren't learning because of ineffective teachers. Gates and others can make this imputation with impunity because teachers—like accused witches—are mostly female.

A few months before Rigoberto saw his life as a teacher as intolerable, President Obama himself justified the wholesale firing of mostly female teachers and counselors at Central Falls High School in Rhode Island because of the school's test scores. The community of Central Falls is plagued by the same problems as Rigoberto's neighborhood. However, in Central Falls as in East Los Angeles, the teachers union got the blame.

The collective punishment of the mostly female staff at Central Falls High reincarnates the wholesale roundup of the mostly female accused witches of Salem. It reincarnates the scapegoating of an entire, vulnerable group for an apparently intractable social problem.

The blaming of teachers for the socioeconomic problems that sabotage student learning recalls the Puritans blaming Salem's female folk healers for deaths caused by male doctors bleeding their patients. The difference is that today it is entire communities that are being bled by social injustice.

The Salem fear of a conspiracy of evil has also been reincarnated. The specific blaming of the teachers unions is merely a reprise of the *fears of evil confederacies of conspiratorial women scheming to harm the young and society.*

And where is it that these modern evil covens meet to concoct their diabolical potions? They meet in what Newsweek calls *"the toxic lunchroom."*[vi] Yes, teachers' lunchrooms are described as *toxic* because teachers there vent about being blamed for society's ills.

Toxic! Poisons! Potions that incapacitate children! The historical parallel is unavoidable. And how are these witches to be dealt with? Newsweek approvingly reports on the power of some principals in Charlotte, North Carolina to "transfer out" up to five teachers from their school, with one of the crimes being "leaders of what principals call 'the toxic lunchroom.'"

So there we have it! In the America of the 21st Century, griping about your boss or his policies will get you banished—the modern equivalent of excommunication—*if* you are in the mostly female profession of teaching. I suppose we should be happy that we are not subject to the gallows!

In 1692, the residents of Salem eyed each other warily after the first accusations, with innocent people wondering if their neighbors would accuse them. Now, the teachers' lounge is similarly gripped with paranoia, with teachers wondering if the formerly friendly colleague next to them might report them as an "obstructionist" (another Newsweek term) subject to exile. Thus, the stress that Rigoberto faced pervaded even his sole place of respite—his lunchroom—during his increasingly stressful days.

Ohio Governor John Kasich would go ever further than North Carolina. During the presidential campaign of 2016, Kasich said that if he were "King of America," he would "abolish *all* teachers' lounges." Why? Because teachers "sit *together* and worry about 'woe is us.'" [vii] If he were the absolute monarch he aspires to be, Kasich would keep the witches separated lest they hatch plots to end their "woe!"

Independent thought and free expression—even in the privacy of the teachers' lounge—are sins to "reformers" like Kasich who would bring authoritarian corporate culture into education. Thus, the covens where such heretical behavior as free expression is practiced must be abolished.

Note Kasich's grossly broad brush. Even if a school was doing well academically, its teachers would lose their lounge. Even if Kasich were making a joke, his proposed satiric blanket punishment is an indictment of all teachers, appalling in its mindless, undiscriminating denunciation.

Such is the way of witch hunting—it does not draw distinctions but instead blames entire groups. The very fact of being a teacher *is* to be a witch, and *all* the witches are guilty. Kasich's dismissive and contemptuous attitude towards this mostly female profession reflects the rank sexism such authorities and the media regularly direct towards teachers.

If you think that Kasich's proposal is unlikely to be implemented, consider the unbelievable actions of Donna Connelly, principal of a Bronx school. Upset with some teachers sitting down, Connelly actually had *all teachers' desks and filing cabinets from the entire school thrown into the trash!*

Teachers were forced to keep their teaching materials in boxes and bags, having to humiliatedly go on the ground and rifle through them in front of students to find teaching materials. The witches were taught a lesson in their individual hovels!

Let us return to those dens of iniquity, teacher lunchrooms. The policies against dissent adopted by North Carolina and proposed by Ohio's governor reveal the blatant double standard of politicians in how they treat teachers versus other workers in fields that are not dominated by women. In male-dominated fields, the workers have a right to complain, a right that the government itself will support.

In supporting the rights of male workers, the National Labor Relations Board (NLRB) itself sued a company that fired an emergency medical technician for criticizing a supervisor on Facebook. According to the NLRB attorney, Lafe Solomon, "It's the same as talking at the water cooler….employees have the protection under the law to talk to each other about conditions at work."

Jonathan Kreisberg, the NLRB director in Hartford, Connecticut went even further and maintained that, "If employees are upset about their supervisor and get together on their own time, talk about him, criticize and call him names, they can do that." [viii]

The NLRB, of course, is an arm of the federal government. This is the same federal government that is pushing the educational "reform" stipulations for schools in distressed communities, stipulations that now apparently include involuntary transfer from a school for anyone suspected of "dissing" the principal during lunch.

Why is there such a double-standard? Why is it okay for an emergency medical technician (EMT) to criticize the boss online, but forbidden for a teacher to criticize a school policy privately during a duty-free lunch? The difference is that most EMTs are male and most teachers are female. *Males have a right to gripe; females have a duty to be persevering and subservient.*

Scourging, Branding, and Excommunication

Female teachers who challenge the sexist stereotype of subservience and do complain are actually *threatened with righteous violence*. One notorious warning was actually issued on the Sabbath. On Sunday August 2, 2015, Governor Chris Christie of New Jersey physically threatened one of the two female leaders of the national teachers unions with a *"punch in the face."* [ix] Christie's specific physical threat mentioned the union. However, this threat of *scourging* was obviously directed against its leaders and members—again, mostly female.

As the reporter Valerie Strauss observes, Christie's threat of a punch in the face is hardly unique; other Republican candidates similarly attacked teachers as *evil enemies of the state*. Wisconsin Governor Scott Walker compared teachers and other public employees who protested against him to *"radical Islamic terrorists!"* Walker maintained that he was capable of taking on the latter as President because of his tough handling of teachers and other public service workers.

Jeb Bush warned that teachers unions were *"super powerful."* He chillingly complained that they controlled education through a government-run "monopoly." Bush exposed the nefarious plots of such unions to slyly resist change through manipulation, i.e., by being "masters of delay and deferral."

Ohio governor John Kasich actually calls for the very Superman of the witch-hunting film we have discussed. This is an education CEO with the power to "override parts of union contracts." The *Education Superman* would thus have the power to undo the spells that incapacitate children during the incantations of the evil witch covens. These evil spells are the words spelled out in union contracts that respect the rights of teachers.

Going back to Rigoberto, it wasn't just his lunch and his workday that was stressful; it was his entire day, including after he left school to go home or to go into his community. For with the online publication of Rigoberto's name as "less-effective," America has revived another tactic from its witch-hunting past—*the public branding of witches or errant women and their humiliation by the entire community*. The purpose of such branding then was the same as it is now—to let the sinner know in her every waking moment that the community knows of her trespass.

In Puritan days, women who were found to be adulterous had to wear the letter "**A**" in bright colors on their clothing for the rest of their lives—a practice made famous by Nathaniel Hawthorne's book, *The Scarlet Letter*. Rigoberto was now similarly on what can only be called *"The Scarlet List"* published by the Los Angeles Times.

Rigoberto must have wondered, "Which of my neighbors has seen me on that list?" As he withdrew money from his local bank or attended church, he had to ask, "Is there someone here who thinks I am *'Less Effective'* in my teaching?"

As he walked home and saw the parents of students, Rigoberto must have worried, "Do they also think I am *'Less Effective'* in my life?" As he greeted casual acquaintances, Rigoberto agonized, "Who believes I am *'Less*

Effective' as a person? Who sees me as *less than a human being*?"

When the Los Angeles Times branded Rigoberto, it in effect *excommunicated* him from the community that he loved.

Inquisitions and Exorcism!

On the very Sunday that Rigoberto jumped into the void, a conference in New York called *Education Nation* was being promoted extensively in the media. Rigoberto undoubtedly watched the promotions for it in the days before his fatal decision.

The teasers for the conference prominently featured *the educational threat*. These promotions portentously proclaimed that noted luminaries across the nation would gravely deliberate on the problem of kids not learning and its deleterious impact on the nation's future.

In blaming teachers for mentally enfeebling children, the conference would be a *replay of the Salem inquests* that were convened to determine who should be indicted for the witchcraft that was obviously bewitching children and causing problems for the colony. It is quite likely that Rigoberto left for the canyon after feeling personally attacked by such dire warnings from the *Education Nation* inquest that came soon after his online branding.

During the conference itself, which began the very day after Rigoberto died, the media prominently reported the accusations of a young female teacher from New York.

She complained that the teachers union was preventing her from teaching more hours for free in order to help students.

This young accuser immediately gained national prominence and admiration. Commentators nodded knowingly. The education consultant on MSNBC exclaimed, "It's a generational divide," claiming thereby that young teachers wanted to help kids but the older ones were preventing them from doing so.

In Salem, it was similarly the young girls like Ann Putnam who accused the alleged old hags in the coven of harming youngsters. Recalling this, we can understand the psychological motivations of this young teacher to denounce older colleagues.

In all witch hunts, when someone who is under suspicion accuses others, the cruel attention is shifted *away* to the newly accused. In this period of trial in education, *all* teachers are under suspicion. Young teachers who have not earned tenure are especially vulnerable and are therefore under pressure to prove their loyalty to the authorities who have power over them.

Some young teachers inevitably succumb to the temptation to denounce others. In Salem itself, much sympathetic and favorable attention was festooned upon young accusers who exposed the evil actions of their older associates—precisely the reward this young accuser of today reaped.

Now, as in 1692, severe crises create a willing and bloodthirsty audience for the show trials like *Education*

Nation. These crises raise formerly unimaginable doubts in a previously confident society. For many, these doubts can only be erased by finding scapegoats to blame. Now, as then, the machinations of apparently conspiratorial groups are blamed—teachers unions now, witches' covens then.

We have seen that many of the leading minds in 16th and 17th Century Europe and America pontificated about the deleterious effects of witches on society. They proposed unassailable tests to determine who was a witch and who should be hounded into non-existence. So now does our national intelligentsia and political leaders grimly ponder the effect of "bad teachers" on the nation.

The similarities are astounding! Our esteemed leaders today gravely propose tests to determine who is a bad teacher. Ambitious politicians and the media scrutinize who should be hounded out of the profession. Finally, powerful Pharisees hound the accused—as in Rigoberto's case—into similar non-existence as the accused witches of Salem.

The most important parallel with Salem, however, lies in the motivations of the accusers. Just as Salem accusers like Putnam stood to gain from the property of the accused, so do many who today accuse teachers of incompetence stand to profit handsomely from their modern form of witch hunting.

On the heels of the accusations of teacher incompetence, educational profiteers rush in with the promotion of tests, materials, and training to "reform" education. They reap huge windfalls as some schools are repeatedly labeled "failing schools" in preparation for them to be privatized.

In addition, those who open charter schools to take over "failing schools" gain access—with very little oversight and accountability—to some of the $400 billion spent annually on education.

Finally, but most importantly for our democracy, those politicians who demonize teachers in order to promote charter schools somehow find that their election campaigns receive substantial donations from the charter school industry.

If, as in Salem, we follow the money behind the rabid rhetoric, we come to an extreme economic philosophy and political movement call **neoliberalism**. *Neoliberalism seeks* to *remove the restrictions from capitalism that protect society and to introduce capitalism into spheres formerly administered by government on behalf of the people.* Neoliberalism is basically reactionary or extremely conservative economics and is therefore different from political liberalism.

Neoliberalism is an aggressive economic movement that has consequently—in various ways—attacked workers, professionals, consumers, and the general citizenry at home and abroad in order to fill the pockets of investors. These investors constantly scour for new areas to secure profits. They thus attack anything—including teachers unions—that stand in their way.

As neoliberal investors seek to profit from education, they fund a movement they call *"education reform."* With copious funds to donate, they find hungry and rabid political lap dogs willing to howl and bark at teachers. Sanctimonious, self-interested *neoliberals* like Jeb

Bush—the Thomas Putnams of today—lead this baying pack of supposed education "reformers" with their attacks on teachers.

The demonizing of teachers, restriction of teachers' rights, and curtailing of democracy in education isn't intended to improve education as "reformers" opportunistically claim. Their simple goal is rather to turn over the education of America's youth to profit makers.

Profits in education can be acquired by destroying any opposition—particularly teachers unions—to the dismantling of the American education system as we know it. We will therefore thoroughly examine neoliberalism in Chapters Six and Seven in order to get to the root of the problem of witch hunts against teachers.

The daily attacks teachers face across the nation are *a national exorcism* similar to that which bedeviled Salem in 1692. The victims are again mostly women, the evidence against them is based on tests, and there is a rabid, community outcry to rid ourselves of those who are harming our youth.

Furthermore, those who incite the crowds stand to benefit from the dispossession of the accused. Our distinguished political and intellectual leaders are made oblivious to reason by the shimmering coin of investors. They enthusiastically and sometimes violently endorse the tests, the trials, and the destruction of lives.

The iconic Irish poet, Yeats, captures the America of today well in his famous poem about Ireland's own bloody chaos during the Easter Rising of 1916:

Turning and turning in the widening gyre
The falcon cannot hear the falconer;
Things fall apart; the centre cannot hold;
Mere anarchy is loosed upon the world,
The blood-dimmed tide is loosed, and everywhere
The ceremony of innocence is drowned.
The best lack all conviction, while the worst
Are full of passionate intensity.

WILLIAM BUTLER YEATS, EXCERPTED FROM
"THE SECOND COMING," 1919

CHAPTER 5

Scapegoating Betrays Hope

WHEN MY KIDS were young, I strongly counseled them from taking up teaching as a profession. Not that they wanted to. My daughter was somewhat inclined to teaching, but even before she became aware of the current witch hunts, she never entertained it as a profession because she observed that her fellow public school students were "mean to teachers." She commented that teachers had little recourse in getting students to behave or study.

Some of you who have never spent a semester teaching and assigning grades might think, "Well, the teacher does have the power of a giving a failing grade to a student who doesn't study for exams or do assigned work. Students would certainly be motivated to work for a better grade."

However, the power and incentive of awarding grades only exists if the student or parent actually cares enough when a student gets a "D" or an "F" *and* cares enough to ensure that the student puts in enough of a learning effort to earn a better grade. Unfortunately, as any teacher can tell you, this is not the case. Any student in a *failing community* (more on those later) could even verify that some students actually take *a perverse pride in failing classes*.

When my son completed his graduate degree in Public Health, it took him some time to get a full-time job in his field. He got a temporary job doing long-term substituting at the middle school he had attended. This experience strongly deterred him from considering teaching as a career.

It wasn't just the behavior and lack of focus of the students that was disconcerting. My son's former teachers, now his colleagues, told him of unreasonable expectations and constant blame coming down from the state headquarters. His former principal, now his boss, confided in him that he too felt the blaming of teachers was unreasonable but that he had to walk a precarious line between being fair to teachers and fulfilling state directives.

These professionals, like the ones at my school and like teachers all across America, are living in a Kafkaesque, absurdist nightmare. It is a nightmare that recurs not only in American history but also throughout the human experience in every human culture.

Exploring the horror of scapegoating beyond Salem— in different places throughout the ages—will help us to better understand its current manifestation at home. Such an analysis involves not only looking at the history but also the literature prompted by scapegoating.

Insights gleaned from the experiences of our ancestors and the wisdom of our poets and writers will help us to fully understand and overcome the current demonization of teachers. Such insights will also help to provide you with the mental fortitude necessary to prevent the future demonization of the group to which *you* belong.

A Hideous History

1. THE WORLD'S CURSE

For the fellow teachers and family of Rigoberto Ruelas Jr., the Kafkaesque absurdity is finding out that someone you love dearly has been scapegoated to his death. This nightmare of the Ruelas family is merely a modern version of that of the medieval Jewish family which finds its father murdered because the Black Death has killed some of the townsfolk and Jews are accused of causing this plague by poisoning the wells. Just as Jews were accused of sabotaging the community then, so are teachers blamed for sabotaging the nation now. The difference is merely one of degree.

American teachers aren't the only ones victimized by such absurdist scapegoating today. In one notable and longstanding case, one nation in the Middle East has been paying for the sins of many in Europe. For Palestinians, the Kafkaesque absurdity is the incomprehensible reality of being dispossessed because they must pay for the crimes of European anti-Semitism throughout the ages.

More generally, the poverty, dislocations, and war that neoliberal capitalism imposes on the "Third World" have created insecure and desperate populations that look for visible culprits. This has resulted in scapegoating becoming a widespread problem around the world.

For Christians and Hindus in Pakistan, the nightmare is having a Muslim mob attack you because your fellow citizens are frustrated with living conditions and US drone attacks. For Muslims in India, it is having a Hindu mob attack you because India's neoliberal, Hindu-nationalist government has dispossessed farmers and uses religion to divert the focus of people's anger. For Pentecostalists in Ethiopia, it is having an Orthodox Christian mob attack you because Ethiopia's neoliberal government pursues policies that hurt the people.

No religion is immune from the tendency to scapegoat the other when its population is under stress. In Palestine's West Bank, Jewish settlers, protected by the Israeli Army, terrorize the daily lives of Palestinians under occupation. In Burma, Buddhists—idealized in the West as being peaceful—have committed genocide against Rohingya Muslims.

In all cases, the mobs, whipped up into a bloodlust by religious fanatics, feel great satisfaction when their victims are punished. Scapegoating can be summed up as *catharsis as cure*, or rather, *attempted* cure.

When scapegoating becomes an official policy, it also affects those with some measure of power, those who must carry out the edicts of scapegoating despite knowing better. Such a conflict of conscience creates moral dilemmas that weigh heavily.

For school principals today, this nightmare dilemma is whether to commend dedicated teachers like Rigoberto Ruelas Jr. or to follow state mandates and enact sanctions against them. State rules often demand such sanctions against teachers labeled "less effective" by impersonal metrics based on tests that their students neither care about nor are equipped to take because of language background.

This nightmare dilemma of conscience is again a modern version of that faced throughout the ages by fairly decent people whose natural sense of right and wrong is compromised by the responsibilities of their authority. The dilemna is that of the czarist police officer, fictionalized in *Fiddler on the Roof*, who knows fully well that the Jews against whom he must conduct a pogrom are innocent, but who must punish a few because of orders from on high.

The theme of the official with a heavy conscience is ancient, and we find it in religious stories. In the Bible, for example, Pontius Pilate knows that Jesus is innocent but feels he must give in to those who want this teacher dead. The phrase "to wash one's hands" of responsibility actually derives from Pilate's futile attempt—by symbolically washing his hands—to avoid personal responsibility for the injustice he is about to commit.

As we have seen, the tendency to find a scapegoat is not just an American trait; it is unfortunately a very human one. This is why it has been a powerful theme in literature and spiritual thought throughout the ages. The very story of Jesus dying on the cross for the sins of humanity reflects this scapegoat theme—the feeling that even in God's eyes, *someone has to pay for sins that have been committed*, regardless of whether it is an innocent person who must face the physical axe, or in this case, the cross.

2. Scapegoating the American Way

Someone has to pay—in every land and at every time! In drawing a historical line from the 1692 persecution in Salem to the current mistreatment of teachers, I am merely following in the footsteps of the great playwright Arthur Miller. In 1953, Miller published *The Crucible*. That play uses the persecution of Salem women in 1692 as a metaphor for the anti-communist hysteria and purges of the 1950s—hysteria that hurt Miller himself and for which writing *The Crucible* was great therapy.

The word "crucible" has two meanings, both essential to Miller's theme. The first meaning is that of *a place or time of extreme test or trial.* This meaning certainly captures the time of ordeal under which teachers work and live today.

The second meaning of "crucible" is that of *a place or situation where different elements give birth to something new.* Miller's story does not actually go past the 1690s and therefore does not explicitly show the recurring witch hunts to which Salem give birth. However, Miller effectively indicted the McCarthyite hysteria of the 1950s. He clearly showed that something macabre took a horrible shape in the Salem of 1692, something that would continue to *haunt the land in times to come.*

Earlier, in a similar vein in 1948, Shirley Jackson wrote a powerful short story called "The Lottery" which superbly captures the essence of scapegoating. Here is an online summary:

> *On a warm day in late June…, villagers gather in the*
> *square to participate in a lottery run by Mr. Summers,*
> *who officiates at all the big civic events. The children*
> *arrive first and begin collecting stones until their par-*
> *ents call them to order. Mrs. Hutchinson arrives late*
> *and chats briefly…*
>
> *Mr. Summers calls each head of the household…*
> *each selects a slip of paper. Once the men have chosen,*
> *Mr. Summers allows everyone to open the paper and*
> *see who has been selected. It is Bill Hutchinson. His wife*
> *immediately starts protesting…*
>
> *There are five people total in the Hutchinson family.*
> *Mr. Summers places five slips of paper into the box and*
> *each member of the family draws. Tess (Mrs. Hutchinson)*
> *draws a slip of paper with a big black dot in the center. Not*
> *good. The villagers advance on her, and it becomes crystal*
> *clear what the prize for the lottery really is: a stoning.*
> *Tess protests in vain as the villagers attack her.* [x]

Jackson was greatly vilified and received a lot of hate mail
for writing this story. Some of the hatred directed at her
was due to the very Americana of the story's setting—
small-town America populated by good, god-fearing, sensible
people. Outraged readers felt that surely we, as respectable
average citizens, would not be capable of such a horrific
act! Moreover, like Miller, Jackson had suggested that such
murderous scapegoating was a regular occurrence. In her
story, the lottery of death occurs *every year!*

When Jackson published her story in 1948, we were one year into the Second Red Scare, more popularly known as the McCarthy Era—the period that Arthur Miller would later indict. The search to find communists in our midst was in full swing. President Truman had already created loyalty boards to *test* the loyalty of government employees.

The House Un-American Affairs Committee had been investigating alleged subversion for a few years. It had even investigated subversion in Hollywood in 1947, resulting in hundreds of artists being blacklisted. That list included Charlie Chaplin, Paul Robeson, and Orson Welles. Like Arthur Miller, they would respond by leaving the country.

Apart from not being able to find work or finding the repressive atmosphere too stifling for free and creative expression, these artists had good cause to actually fear for their physical safely. Despite a lack of evidence, the FBI under J. Edgar Hoover listed Orson Welles as a Communist. His name was placed on the Agency's Security Index, which was originally called the *Custodial Detention Index*.

As indicated by the name of the government list, alleged subversives on it would be *rounded up* whenever the FBI assessed that there was a national emergency. One might ask: rounded up for what? Prior to being hanged, the accused women of Salem were also rounded up. Is it too much of a stretch to point out that Hitler started by rounding up communists in response to the burning of the Reichstag in 1933?

The anti-communist hysteria of the McCarthy Era that led to the "round up" lists was most popular in the small-town America depicted by Shirley Jackson in *The Lottery*. It was here that opportunistic politicians like Richard Nixon had been most effective in whipping people into a frenzy of fear to root out the innocuous-looking evildoers in our midst.

After being threatened by Congressional investigation, Hollywood participated in this witch hunting by producing films with such lurid titles as *The Red Menace* and *I Married a Communist*. Even your husband or wife was not to be trusted!

In the 1950s, the mass media promoted a fear that, not unsurprisingly, resulted in a mass hysteria. Some lost their jobs; others lost their lives. The film *Trumbo* depicted this era well. Is it much different today? For Rigoberto Ruelas Jr., it was not.

Obama Scapegoats—Scientifically

Today, Americans feel that hysteria and scapegoating only occur in benighted places among backward peoples with fundamentalist religions. They believe that in our country itself, such irrational cruelty is merely an unfortunate phenomenon of the past.

The problem, of course, lies in the difficulty of looking at oneself honestly. It is usually only with hindsight and the lack of emotional and social involvement that we can recognize the hysteria that is central to scapegoating.

As long as we are emotionally removed, it is not difficult to see such failings in other places and at other times in our own history.

In contrast, at the very moment when we are seized by the fears caused by distressing events, our anxieties wrench our emotions. These alarmed emotions overpower our intellect. They prompt us to stampede along with the fearful herd. Our emotional and social involvement with unsettling issues prevents us from realizing that we are scapegoating innocents, for our disturbed minds cannot see reality for what it is.

1. A SCIENTIFIC VENEER

The explanation for the persistence of scapegoating in the midst of our modernity is that, as Karen Armstrong indicates, education and modernity are no guarantees against such a primeval, atavistic urge to find the culprit. Today, we merely see our search for wrongdoers as a very natural and sensible solution to the very real problems we face.

Modernity, however, does play a role in determining *the nature* of modern scapegoating. To justify our irrational responses to social problems, we coat these reactions with **a scientific veneer.** After all, in 1692—at the dawn of the Scientific Age—the inhabitants of Salem and Massachusetts actually thought that they were practicing the most modern of science in their pursuit of witches!

Thus, as in Salem, we just don't grab and lynch the malefactors; instead we go through *a process of testing* to prove that our victims are guilty and that the punishments are justified. We abuse the processes and language of science to justify that most ancient of sins in the tribe—the casting out of the innocent in a collective catharsis.

Moreover, as we will see later, *there are modern, secular ideologies that lend themselves just as much to fanaticism and scapegoating* as Puritanism did in Salem and as religion continues to do in other countries. Such a modern, "scientific" ideology—*neoliberalism*—drives the move to "reform" education.

Furthermore, as in Salem, the flames of this ideology are spread by those who have much baser interests than they propound. The prospect of obtaining education money currently paid to the old wives in the teachers unions elicits licked lips among the avaricious in the same manner that the land of the old maids in Salem caught the scheming eye of Thomas Putnam. The difference is that whereas Putnam used religious Puritan ideology against Salem women, education "reformers" today use economic neoliberal ideology against female teachers.

Knowing how the dedicated teacher Rigoberto Ruelas Jr. was fatally affected by an agenda-driven scapegoating and knowing how good teachers have become severely demoralized and even clinically depressed by it, I fear for the mental health of my own students should they become teachers.

Like my colleagues, I discourage not only my own children but also my students from entering the teaching profession in the current climate. Indeed there have been studies indicating that both the number and quality of students entering teacher training programs have diminished because of society's continual baiting of teachers like Rigoberto.

2. Denying Persecution

Rigoberto Ruelas Jr. should have been the canary in the mine. His death should have served as a wake-up call to our nation to be fair to teachers and not blame them for the ills of society that are reflected in education. Teachers, like cops, have to deal with these ills but neither teachers nor cops can cure such problems of society by themselves.

However, Rigoberto's death has been treated just like the deaths of those accused of witchcraft in 17th Century Europe and America who killed themselves rather than face continuing scorn and torture. Like those suicides of old, Rigoberto's only exit from his pain has been virtually ignored.

Whereas the witch hunters of Salem and Europe made a grand spectacle of putting on trial and executing those they arrested for witchcraft, they quietly ignored those distressed souls who drank poison, jumped into rivers, or plunged knives into their chests rather than endure the ridicule, torment, and torture of being accused of witchcraft. The current witch hunters—whether the media or politicians—have done the same with Rigoberto's death.

A comparison of two suicides illustrates how the media dismisses the pain caused by the hounding of teachers. On September 22, 2010, Tyler Clementi, a Rutgers student, jumped off the George Washington Bridge connecting

New Jersey and New York because his roommate taped and broadcast him having gay sex. The media covered Tyler's death extensively—as well as it should have because Tyler suffered heinous bullying. The media also did not equivocate about the cause of his death—the embarrassment caused by having his sex acts publicly displayed on the internet.

As we have learned, Rigoberto also jumped—just *four* days after Tyler. And the reason was the same: embarrassment on the internet. However, Rigoberto's death was hardly mentioned.

Moreover, in contrast to Tyler's death, the scant coverage of Rigoberto's death always insisted that "there is never just one reason why someone commits suicide." This caveat was *never* raised in the coverage of Tyler's suicide. The purpose of raising the caveat is therefore to deflect media responsibility for the humiliating online branding of Rigoberto as a "less effective" teacher by the media itself.

3. Witch-Finders on the Hunt

The only sense in which there was "not just one reason" for Rigoberto's suicide is this: there were numerous other ways in which Rigoberto, like other teachers, felt bullied and demeaned for being a teacher. Just prior to Rigoberto's death, Bill Gates and the producer of *Waiting for Superman* denigrated public schools and their teachers. Even a so-called "financial guru" got in on the act. Suzie Orman declared that teachers shouldn't be teaching finance because they could never teach financial empowerment due to their inevitable low self-esteem caused by being underpaid.

There was also the continual denigration of teachers in the media by columnists and editorialists intent on promoting charter schools. In an article introducing the database on "teacher effectiveness" that depressed Rigoberto, the Los Angeles Times declared its intention in the subtitle to *"look at which educators help students learn and which hold them back."* [xi]

According to the database, Rigoberto was thus impeding the success of the kids he loved dearly. The highest education official in the land, Secretary of Education Arne Duncan, enthusiastically endorsed this database and its publication in August 2010, despite the prescient warning by the Los Angeles teachers union that such publication was irresponsible and dangerous.

4. BETRAYAL

The most hurtful blow of all to Rigoberto had to be that coming from President Obama. Obama's justification of the wholesale firing of teachers and counselors at Central Falls High School in Rhode Island was nothing less than the sanctioning of a bloodless educational pogrom.

The hurt was that the teachers with the most difficult students in the most difficult neighborhoods were going to be *blamed for the conditions of their work.* The hurt was that the most important person in the land, a man to whom teachers looked up because he had risen from adversity in the same way that they hope their students would rise from adversity, had condemned them because of the very adversity their students faced.

For Rigoberto, the psychic pain was obviously unbearable. I know, because Obama's cruel, offhand justification of the Central Falls purge hit me in the gut and depressed me even though my evaluations are satisfactory. Obama's insult, in its casual, cold, arrogant manner, had the same effect on my colleagues at the school where I teach and obviously on the besieged teachers at Central Falls.

For Rigoberto, the pain had to be worse. He had attended the school at which he worked. He had come from the same deprived background as his students. However, unlike his fellow classmates and most of his students, Rigoberto had believed and had acted on the sweet promise made by the system—the promise that if he studied hard and worked hard, he could have a decent life.

And so Rigoberto studied hard and worked hard. He became a teaching assistant at the tough school he had attended. He didn't stop there. With the promise of a better life in mind, he continued to study and work to become a teacher, dedicating his life to those who reminded him of himself at a younger age.

Rigoberto did succeed in inspiring some to rise out of the conditions of their neighborhood—just as he himself had done. However, this mattered not to those who pored over the results of his students' standardized tests—just as the upright lives of many of the accused Salem women mattered not to the honorable judges poring over the results of the tests for witchcraft.

Rigoberto's upright and dedicated life mattered not because, like the Salem judges, the Los Angeles Times was looking for scapegoats. Those who scour the land for scapegoats in America don't let facts get in the way—much like the mobs in Pakistan intent on rooting out the infidels.

The relevant facts that would stop scapegoating if they were honestly examined are the sociological effects of poverty on education. A few individuals in a disadvantaged community, Rigoberto for example, can indeed break out of poverty. However, the entire community cannot.

Rigoberto could inspire a few of his students to similarly escape their condition, but most could not. The burden of poverty weighs on students' preparation, motivation, and educational resources. Not everyone has the extraordinary qualities to overcome the obstacles of family, neighborhood, material, and language handicaps. More importantly, nor does the competitive economy permit a large-scale breaking out of poverty.

Like most of his classmates, Rigoberto's own students could not *as a group* break out of the poverty awarded by their birth without profound social change that addressed the handicaps that accompanied such poverty. Teachers will be able to overcome some of the effects of poverty for some students. However, for all of the effects of poverty to be eliminated for all students—which is what the education commissars now demand—*poverty itself has to be addressed.*

The necessity of addressing poverty through social justice is a simple sociological fact that no amount of sloganeering can change. And even when, by dint of extraordinary effort, a person like Rigoberto manages to break out of this poverty in order to help others, he finds that the society and government blames him—the educational worker—for the deleterious educational effects of the society's injustice towards those who are left behind.

Betrayed by the system he had been led to believe in and also betrayed by a leader, Obama, who had promised "Hope" for the underprivileged like himself, Rigoberto must have felt that his life had become as useless as the "*less effective*" term employed by the Los Angeles Times implied. And so he acted accordingly.

5. A Presidential Precedent for Trump

The day after Rigoberto jumped, while his body lay broken, cold, and alone at the bottom of a ravine in the canyon, Obama told Matt Lauer on NBC *Today* show, "*We've got to be able to identify teachers….and…if some teachers aren't doing a good job, **they've got to go**.*" [xii]

Obama advocated firing teachers in the same offhand manner that Trump fired his apprentices. Obama criticizes Trump now. However, Obama's scapegoating attitude presaged and prepared the way for Trump's present attacks on the vulnerable.

Rigoberto beat Obama to it by a day. He had picked up on the condemnatory attitude of society, the media, Obama, and guests on *Oprah*. Obama was as responsible for the death of Rigoberto Ruelas Jr. as much as the Puritan officials of Salem were for the death of Giles Corey.

Let's develop the analogy further. In 1692, Salem officials piled rocks on the chest of the aged Giles Corey until his ribs broke, rendering his lungs useless. In our time, Arne Duncan—picked by Obama as Education Secretary despite warnings about his callous attitude—selected the heavy bricks of impossible goals and consequential humiliation. Then Barack Hussein Obama placed these bricks on Rigoberto's chest until this teacher's spirit broke, rendering his life as useless as the Los Angeles Times designation had indicated.

Not a Teacher? You're Next!

Each of us should spread the ignored story of Rigoberto Ruelas Jr. It sometimes takes a specific victim—a particular outrage—to raise consciousness in the minds of individuals and to create a paradigm shift. The deaths of the nine Charlestown church victims have, for example, finally moved the South to deal honestly with the issue of the Confederate flag.

Although difficult, combating scapegoating in a society that is engaged in the mindless pursuit of culprits is possible if one listens, really listens, to the stories of the victims. In listening to the victims, we may also perhaps eventually realize how scapegoating harms even the perpetrators and the bystanders.

Learning is therefore the antidote to scapegoating. The basic purpose of education is to learn how to deal more effectively with the world in which we live. This is why literature and history are an integral part of the curriculum.

The stories and verses of the past help us to realize that what we are facing today—the seeming intractable problems—has been faced before by other individuals and peoples. The knowledge derived from familiarity with our cultural heritage thus gives us the firm grounding that helps to prevent us from being blown whichever way the prevailing wind blows.

Those shifting winds are the powerful gusts of popular fads and prejudices, the madness of the crowds. Our literature and history lend us an intellectual and emotional stability that immunizes us against popular hysteria like scapegoating.

A particular bit of literature and history could again help here. John Donne (1572–1631) lived during a time of murderous religious wars involving horrible massacres such as those committed during the Thirty Years War (1618–1648). Perhaps inspired by a revulsion against such barbarity, he penned insightful meditations that powerfully capture our human interconnectedness.

"Meditation 17," is the most well-known of Donne's reflections:

Meditation 17

No man is an island,
Entire of itself;
Every man is a piece of the continent,

A part of the main.
If a clod be washed away by the sea,
Europe is the less,
As well as if a promontory were,
As well as if a manor of thy friend's or of thine own
were:
Any man's death diminishes me,
Because I am involved in mankind.
Therefore, send not to know for whom the bell tolls;
It tolls for thee.

JOHN DONNE, 1624.

In a similar vein, speaking of segregation and injustice to blacks, Martin Luther King insightfully pointed out that such injustice harms not only African Americans but also the whites who perpetrate it. It creates psychic distortions in the consciousness, personalities, and characters of the perpetrators. It essentially makes them less happy, or as King would put it, less close to God. This same principle applies to those who would scapegoat teachers for the ills of society.

In the next chapter, "Destroying American Professionalism," we will discover a more concrete effect of scapegoating teachers on those who are not themselves educators. We will see precisely how the work bell—not the class bell—does indeed toll for you, the non-teacher.

You may never set foot in a classroom to teach but you will nevertheless be confronted with the impossible conditions of work that teachers are having to endure now. The same force—*neoliberalism*—that is destroying teachers, schools, and education now will be targeting your workplace next!

CHAPTER 6

— ๑ —

Destroying American Professionalism

First they came for the Communists,
And I did not speak out—because I was not a Communist.

Then they came for the Socialists,
And I did not speak out—because I was not a Socialist.

Then they came for the trade unionists,
And I did not speak out—because I was not a trade unionist.

Then they came for the Jews,
And I did not speak out—because I was not a Jew.

Then they came for me,
And there was no one left to speak out for me!

PASTOR MARTIN NIEMOLLER, GERMANY, 1946

Teachers: Canaries in the Mine

THE DEATH OF Rigoberto Ruelas Jr. is a harbinger of the impending death of America's professional class. Not the entire class, however, just the vast majority of it. Rigoberto's death is more accurately an omen of the death of the professional classes with the exception of those deemed to be important because they protect society's injustice with a gun or with a pen.

Combating scapegoating against teachers is therefore not just a disinterested, humanitarian thing to do on behalf of others. A society that begins to scapegoat one group will eventually scapegoat others in turn—until it scapegoats the group to which *you* belong.

American teachers are themselves suffering now because they did not speak out against the scapegoating of others—the workers of America. The scapegoating of America's blue collar workers—for reasons that we will explore later—began in the 1980s. Politicians and the media blamed them for the failure of American businesses. Workers were punished by the weakening of their unions and reductions in benefits, pay, and conditions of work.

And what was the attitude of American teachers to this campaign to degrade the American worker? Although some teachers did oppose unfair measures against workers, others let their comfortable, professional middle-class lives distance them from the interests of the fading blue collar workers.

Comfortable in their privilege, some teachers denigrated the gritty workers and their militant unions. As Pastor Niemoller would say, the teachers let the authorities come for the workers and their unions, not realizing that they and their right to associate would be next.

To understand what has been happening to teachers as professionals today is thus to understand what has already happened to workers and what has been happening somewhat more subtly to other professionals in America. As the least respected professionals, teachers occupy the middle ground between blue-collar workers and other white-collar professionals.

The campaign against America's workers has already succeeded. If the similarly brutal campaign against teachers is successful, the presently more moderate pressure against other professionals will morph into the outrageous measures currently directed at teachers. As canaries in the mine of professionals, the fate of teachers will predict your fate as a professional.

Understanding the dynamics endangering professionals today requires us to examine the motive force behind those dynamics. This in turn necessitates that we look at the history of professionalism in capitalist society, including its glorious rise. More importantly, as we examine the current decline of professionals and workers, we will better understand much of the turmoil in our political system, including the rise of demagogues like Trump.

Digging deeper, it also becomes absolutely important to understand what *neoliberalism* (a fancy term for an old concept) really is and *to see the connection between neoliberalism and "education reform."* Once we do so, we will understand both the agenda behind the attacks on teachers as well as the broader threat to other professionals.

The Rise of Professionalism

The professional classes as we know them today developed with the rise of early capitalism, called mercantile capitalism, in Europe during the 1500s. In the West, the full story of capitalism's emergence has remained hidden from the vast majority of the public in order to hide its intrinsically exploitative and violent nature.

The following history is thus absolutely important in assessing whether more capitalism—e.g., privatization and educational choice— will actually solve the problems in education.

1. Capitalism: A Savage Birth

The very emergence and continued success of mercantile capitalism was dependent on Europe's exploitation of its new colonies in the Americas and Asia and on the labor of enslaved Africans.

The wealth looted from Mexico and South America (and extracted by enslaving Native Americans) provided the basis for currency in Europe in the form of gold and silver. With currency now available, European trade could explode. The first European sea traders in the 1500s simply bought spices and other desirable items from Asians to resell in Europe. (The form of payment, of course, was the coined precious metals stolen from Native Americans.)

Soon, however, the Europeans created trading-post empires in Asia similar in intent to the larger land empires they had created in the Americas. The model learned from subjugating Native Americans was now applied to Asians.

Armed with modern weapons and their private armies, Europeans forced Asians to supply them with desired items for lower and lower prices, eventually creating plantations, for example, with coerced native labor.

Back in the Americas, slave plantations using enslaved Africans were created. The successful trade in the products—notably sugar—produced by these immiserated humans was intrinsic to the success and development of early capitalism. Slavery became just as important as the domination of the Asian trade and the robbery and subjugation of Native Americans. The successful birth of European capitalism was therefore *dependent on the domination and exploitation of the people on three continents.*

Thus, those who argue that capitalism is based on free trade are either woefully or willfully ignorant. Capitalism was born out of the immiserating of Native Americans, Asians, and Africans. These groups were *not allowed any freedom* to trade their land, labor, precious metals, or products as they wished.

Capitalism further developed, in its industrial stage, through the immiseration of European peasants and workers. This intrinsically problem-causing nature of capitalism is certainly relevant to point out to those who call for a free market in education, believing it will be a panacea for education problems.

Capitalism will not solve the problems in education. Rather, by generating social stratification and the evils inherent in poverty, capitalism has actually *caused* the problems we face today in education. The continuing cause of a chronically severe social ill can certainly not be its solution.

2. Working for the Man

Let us return to early capitalism and the development of the professional class. We have seen that capitalism created new trading enterprises and required the creation of overseas empires to supply it with coinage and the products necessary for trade. Out of this was born the basic element of capitalism, the corporation.

The first corporations were joint-stock companies, organized to pool resources for the Asian trade. Some of these enterprises, such as the British East India Company, later functioned as actual governments in the trading-post empires. These private-enterprise mini-empires were complete with armies and war-making ability, the latter necessary to ensure the cooperation of local rulers and natives in the quest for products such as spices to trade. Both at home in Europe and in the colonies, these enterprises would be *managed by a new class of professionals.*

Note that in Asia and Africa, political colonialism *followed* economic colonialism and only supplanted it when the latter ran into problems—as when, for example, Indians rebelled against the British East India Company in 1857. Political colonialism developed to protect the interests of the earlier economic colonialism.

This support that the early European state gave to its aggressively expansionist capitalist enterprises still explains politics in our time. It is why politicians today continue to

pursue the economic interests of capitalists both domestically (e.g., in privatizing education) and in foreign policy
(e.g., in pursuing wars to secure resources and investment
opportunities). Such has always been the purpose of the
modern political state in its present form.

The new complex world of colonialism and mercantile
capitalism required the development of a class that could
do the specialized work required by this new economy.
Someone had to keep track of slave purchases. Officials
were needed to administer the trading post empires in Asia
and the land empires in the Americas. Others were needed
to mete out punishment to recalcitrant natives in Asia or to
oversee slavery in the Americas (not the slaves themselves,
but the system).

Private-enterprise colonialism was wild and savage but
it did need a veneer of respectability with the imprimatur
of the government. The government thus needed its own
professional class working in the empires to administer the
political arrangements necessitated by the economic slave
system.

Back in Europe, skilled professionals were needed
in the growing local capitalist enterprises. Accountants,
for example, had to keep the books in order. The class
of professionals grew as these new capitalist enterprises
in Europe experienced wild success due to the coercive
nature of the colonialism on which they depended.

The more brutal the colonialism in the colony, the
more the mother country in Europe had products to trade
and coinage with which to trade them—the necessary

elements of early capitalism. Consequently, the more brutal the colonialism was, the more people in the mother country who could join the professional class working in the capitalist system.

Skilled professionals were also needed in government at home, the newly powerful national governments. Capitalists hated the myriad rules and divisions of the various old feudal economic and political entities, all of which impeded trade. The increasingly wealthy capitalists thus funded—through taxes—the growth of the monarch's power at the expense of that of the nobles. To control the nobles, the monarch kept them at his palace, amusing them with lavish balls and court gossip. The far realms that were once administered by this noble class were now administered by civil servants—professional bureaucrats—in the employ of the king.

Both the economic complexity of capitalism and its required political unity therefore necessitated the growth of the professional class. At the same time, the wealth generated by capitalism's coercive colonial system allowed this class to be compensated relatively decently. Being small in number, educated, and possessing skills vital to the smooth functioning of capitalism and its government of monarchs, professionals were treated and compensated much better than laborers and even skilled workers.

In mercantile and later forms of capitalism, the new professional classes in both government and private industry formed a useful social and political buffer. Professionals became an important part of the growing middle class—sandwiched between the newly ascending capitalist class and the workers and peasants at the bottom.

The fabulously wealthy capitalists and their spokesmen in academia and the media could point to professionals and tell complaining workers and peasants that they only needed to pull themselves up by their bootstraps to be similarly successful. It is a familiar refrain that we still hear today.

Somehow, disadvantaged students today from failing communities savaged by capitalism are supposed to also pull themselves up by their bootstraps as their schools are starved of necessary funds. The origins of both our problems and the excuses that the rich and powerful make for them go way back.

3. Placating Professionals
In time, European capitalists shifted from forcibly procuring items from Asia to producing goods themselves. Thus was born the Industrial Revolution. Starting in the 1700s, mercantile capitalism gave way to industrial capitalism. *The viciousness that capitalism had directed towards Native Americans, Africans, and Asians was now also visited upon European peasants and workers.*

European peasants were kicked off the land they had farmed for a thousand years to make way for enterprises more suitable to the new industrial economy. In England, for example, the peasants were replaced by sheep, with the wool being sent to the factories to feed the new machines of the growing textile industry.

Many white workers in the factories of Europe and the American North fared little better than the blacks on the plantations of the American South. As Pastor Niemoller points out, when you tolerate injustice against others, it eventually comes to be directed against you.

The logic of capitalism is to increase profits at all costs. It should come as little surprise, therefore, that its dynamic is to become increasingly more vicious to people and the environment. For a while under industrial capitalism, it seemed that capitalist society was actually cleaving into two extremes—the industrialists and the workers—and that professionals would be inexorably thrown into the latter class as capitalists sought to extricate maximum profits. Dickens' classic story *A Christmas Carol* illustrates the viciousness of capitalism at the height of the industrial revolution. At this point, many believed that communist revolutions, as Marx had predicted, would sweep the West.

Between 1830 and 1905, there were indeed many socialist and communist revolutions in Europe but none was successful. Why? Western capitalist countries were able to avert communist revolution by bettering the living conditions of their professionals and eventually their workers. Not inclined to give up their own share of existing profits, capitalists placated the classes beneath them with profits obtained from expanding their economies more intensively into the "Third World" or the Global South.

Thus was born the Age of Imperialism (1870-1914). Fantastic profits in the West were generated by controlling third world resources necessary for Western factories and by using colonies as captive markets for the industrial products created by those factories. Western capitalist countries were therefore able to improve the conditions of their professional classes and their working class, staving off the very real threat of communist revolution or radical socialist reform.

After the Russian Revolution of 1917, communism was no longer a theoretical system. The greatest "threat" posed by the Soviet Union to the capitalists who controlled policy in the West was the threat that discontented workers in the West might carry out a similar revolution. However, seeing their lives continually improve and knowing that their children's lives would be even better, the Western professional and working classes continued to shun both revolution and radical reform.

Capitalism Threatens Professionals

Two developments have converged to shatter the friendly co-existence that existed between professionals and the capitalist system. As the world changed, capitalists began to look at professionals differently.

1. TRIUMPH AND CHALLENGE

One dramatic change affecting professionals and workers was the fall of the Soviet Union. When the Soviet Union dissolved in the early 1990s, it removed the threat of a socialist alternative. In the West and especially America, the capitalists who shaped policy no longer had to worry as much about pleasing the classes beneath them.

After the fall of Communism, if the working and professional classes in the West became disgruntled they would certainly not turn to a now-discredited socialism. Western capitalist countries could thus return to squeezing their professionals and workers, proclaiming that this was the way of a free labor market in a free enterprise system, which was now the only game in town.

The second development that would cause capitalists to change their attitude towards professionals began earlier. As countries of the Global South fought for and achieved independence after World War Two, Western economies were affected. Although some developing countries—particularly in Latin America—could still be controlled economically through CIA machinations and military interventions, others managed to gain control over their own resources and economies.

Two important countries in the Global South were large and strong enough to be fairly immune to the CIA and Western military invasion. These were India and China. With independence (India, 1947) and revolution (China, 1949), these countries were able to slowly build back their economies that had been ravaged by centuries of European colonialism and imperialism.

With India under democratic socialism, China under communism, and many other Asian and African countries following suit with similar programs, western capitalists were shut out from economies that leaders of the Global

South had closed in order to throw off the dependence on the Western economies. These leaders were determined to use their countries' resources and economies to benefit the people at home rather than to enrich Europe and North America.

The West was seriously affected by the assertion of political and economic independence by the developing world. Britain has fallen steadily as a world power since it lost India. The same goes for France with its loss of Indochina and African colonies. For Western capitalists, there was therefore dramatically less profit to be made from the "Third World" and, consequently, less largesse to share with the professional and working classes back home.

2. IMPERIALISM DECLINES

Western professionals did not suffer immediately from the decline of imperialism. To compensate for the economic loss of its colonies, Western Europe turned to economic integration—the European Economic Community—that increased trade *within* Europe. Europe also reaped the peace dividend from giving up its historical internecine warfare.

The United States also similarly benefitted from being the sole industrial power left intact after World War Two. It was also able to maintain its control over Latin American economies through interventions that used the supposed "communist threat" as a pretext. These compensatory factors allowed Western Europe and the United States to actually prosper in the 1950s and 1960s and for their professionals to continually raise their standard of living.

The loss of colonies would eventually have an even greater and unanticipated effect, however. India and China would eventually open up their economies—but only to compete with the West in the international market. Western capitalists are presently losing great market share of light industrial products to China and informational technology to India. *With each such blow it receives from those it once dominated abroad, Western capitalism turns the screws on those it still dominates at home.*

In other areas of the world, the ability of Middle Eastern and other oil-producing nations to control their own energy production and prices also put a severe dent in the global capitalist system in the 1970s. No longer could cheap sources of energy be guaranteed by controlling other people's oil.

Similarly, starting in the 1990s, Latin America began declaring its independence from the United States. After the fall of the Soviet Union in the early 1990s, The USA could no longer use the pretext of the "communist threat" to control Latin American economies. Dictatorships that had been installed by the CIA were replaced by reformist socialist governments that were determined to use Latin economies to benefit the Latin people.

For Western capitalists, the increased costs of oil production and the loss of control of the Latin American economies were additional factors that would require drastic changes at home.

3. GIVEBACKS!

As Western capitalists lost control over the world economy, they demanded that their professional and working classes make do with less. For capitalists, compensating these classes decently was no longer possible since such compensation could seriously affect their own anticipated reduced bottom line. Western workers and professionals would have to start agreeing to *"givebacks,"* to give up the benefits awarded to them when imperialism was rampant in Latin America, when the Soviet Union provided the threat of an alternative, and before India and China picked themselves up off the imperialist floor.

This process of demanding givebacks has been occurring in both private and public occupations. In the latter, capitalists demanded tax cuts from the government, which would have to be paid for by reduced wages, fewer benefits, and deteriorating conditions of work for civil service professionals. Regarding teachers, one clever way to reduce pay was to demand that it be tied to improvement in test scores.

Another indirect giveback demanded by Western capitalists was again the reduction of their taxes, this time through drastic cutbacks to the welfare state. These cutbacks would also have severe consequences for professionals and the working class. It was in the 1970s that Western capitalism began to face the economic consequences of the Global South asserting its rights to control its own resources. During that decade, corporate interests therefore started supporting candidates who would "roll back the welfare state" and pursue aggressive military action to control resources in the Global South.

The rollback of social democracy, not surprisingly, would involve the successful candidates cutting taxes for the corporations and wealthy individuals who had funded their political campaigns. This meant eliminating the jobs of government professionals, especially those charged with monitoring the abuses of capitalism. The era of Reagan and Thatcher began. It was an era that would introduce the neoliberalism and austerity that still afflicts us today.

Laissez-Faire—The Toxic Root

Neoliberalism is just a fancy, technical-sounding, new name for something that is very old—*the unrestricted, old-fashioned laissez-faire capitalism of the 1800s.* As we shall see, this unregulated capitalism has a deserved reputation for producing great disparities of wealth and poverty.

1. LOWER TAXES AND DAMAGED KIDS

If there is one news item that illustrates the jarring social contradictions that the advocates of neoliberalism and austerity are trying to re-create, it would be the following one. First of all, let us look at what one governor wants to do:

> *[Florida] Gov. Rick Scott wants...$1 billion in business-friendly tax cuts.... [He] wants to permanently repeal the corporate income tax...*

Next, let's look at what needs to be done with the money that Scott wants to save for businesses:

> *Florida expects a projected surplus of $635 million next year, but state economists say most of the money is needed to pay for higher Medicaid caseloads and more students in public schools, state colleges and universities.*
>
> *…Florida's services for poor and disabled children are so underfunded that they violate federal laws…. Florida's prison system [has]… staff shortages so severe that corrections officers are in physical danger.*
>
> *State agencies [cite]…rampant employee turnover [because of] low pay for child-abuse investigators…. [There is] widespread abuse and violence in Florida's mental institutions…* [xiii]

Note the direct connection between *tax cuts* for businesses and the *underfunding of public education* and other essential services. Reagan and Thatcher are gone, but their followers like Governor Rick Scott of Florida continue chopping away at those services essential to maintaining the social fabric of the nation.

Neoliberal governments lay waste to government, reducing its leavening powers on capitalist society. They invoke economic doctrine in a saintly manner, masking their service to economic masters. For the general public and for workers and professionals in public as well as private employment, the advent of neoliberalism and austerity was the beginning of a nightmare that is simply getting more horrible.

For parents in Flint, Michigan today, the horror is that their children will most certainly be brain-damaged. They will be brain-damaged because of the Tea-Party, venture capitalist governor Rick Snyder. Snyder had his *Emergency Manager* henchman switch Flint water's supply because of austerity—to save money for his $15 million in neoliberal tax cuts for the wealthy and businesses. *American children will be thus be growing up brain-damaged so that neoliberal capitalists can be even richer.*

2. The Lion's Jungle Theory

Neoliberalism is a revival of the philosophy and practice of laissez-faire capitalism that was discredited by the "see no evil" attitude of the Republican presidents of the 1920s such as Hoover. The French phrase *laissez-faire* in effect means "leave alone" or "let it be."

The basic idea of laissez-faire and neoliberalism is that *government should interfere as little as possible in the economy* (including taxation, welfare, and other spending) because any problems in capitalism will naturally be solved through the supposedly self-correcting dynamics inherent in the system itself.

Although laissez-faire thinking goes back to ancient China (with the term being merely a translation of a Taoist concept), the principle really started to become popular as capitalism expanded in Europe during the 1600s and 1700s. As they had earlier done with feudal laws, capitalists began to oppose the national laws of the monarchs who had once been their allies but whose own restrictions now interfered with their trade as the latter expanded and became more complex.

This capitalist opposition to restrictive laws grew as mercantile capitalism transitioned into industrial capitalism during the 1700s and 1800s. During this time, Western capitalists began to produce more of their own products in factories instead of merely being the middlemen for Asian products. This increased production made international trade and the dismantling of trade restrictions more important.

In economically dominant countries like England and France, economic thinkers emerged whose free-market, laissez-faire theories reflected the interests of their industrialist class. These thinkers were called *liberals* (no relationship to today's political liberals) because of their belief in free trade. (*Neoliberalism* gets its name because it is a revival of this classic, laissez-faire *economic liberalism*.)

In England during the Industrial Revolution, factory owners opposed restrictive tariffs against grain imports (the Corn Laws) that protected domestic farmers whose prices were higher. For industrialists, if their workers could have access to cheaper bread made from cheaper imported wheat, these employees could then be paid less.

Leading industrial powers also promoted laissez-faire because they desired to export their products to countries with weaker industries that had protectionist laws. *Thus, selfish, material motives were transformed by the capitalists and their theorists into natural, universal, selfless, and almost religious principles.*

Powerful capitalists thus fought for the removal of government restrictions at home and abroad to allow free trade and laissez-faire. The world's economic lions found a theory that would help then devour their weaker rivals.

3. A LION TAMER BRAVES THE JUNGLE

Historical examples of how selfish motives were promoted as neutral, universal, and natural free-market laws are important to keep in mind as we debate whether to support public schools or to promote "school choice." While the latter sounds like a nice principle of freedom that is beyond reproach, the alert citizen should wonder what baser motives might be behind the insistent proclamation of such an apparently idealistic educational principle.

And baser motives indeed they are! As we shall see, educational "reform" is merely the effort to graft neoliberal, laissez-faire principles onto education. This is precisely why we are exploring the history of laissez-faire: to show that it has not been the panacea that school choice advocates make it out to be.

The problems that we see today with educational privatization are not an accident; *they have their antecedents in the past abuses of laissez-faire, reincarnated in one form now as "educational reform."* Our best defense for public education therefore lies in the facts of history that disprove the neoliberal assumptions and theory behind educational "reform."

The principles of laissez-faire were at work during the Gilded Age of the late 1800s. And indeed, laissez faire does work for a while—for some. During this time, business expanded, creating unimagined wealth for a few. However, those who toiled to produce this wealth worked and lived in misery, a situation documented by the muckraking journalist Upton Sinclair at the turn of the 20th Century in his shocking *expose* appropriately titled *The Jungle*. Sinclair also showed that with non-existent government regulation, consumers were saddled with food products that were simply disgusting—including the flesh of humans who had died in the meatpacking factories!

Jacob Riis, another muckraker, did for housing what Sinclair had done for food. In *How the Other Half Lives*, he exposed the squalor of the tenements where the workers of industry lived. He also wrote about the hopelessness in the lives of the children of these ghettoes in *The Children of the Poor* and *The Children of the Tenements*. Riis' books contain many horrifying pictures of suffering children that give the lie to the laissez faire, neoliberal claim that unrestricted capitalism benefits everyone.

Teachers today, however, should have one piece of praise for the industrialist robber barons of that bygone era. At least the latter did not blame teachers for the failure of immiserated children to learn! The rich and powerful at that time did not pretend to care about educating the poor and the working class.

Unfortunately, the vast majority of politicians in the late nineteenth century also did not consider the misery of children to be the gauge for determining whether an economy was successful; for them, it was rather the expansion of business. By their standards, therefore, laissez-faire seemed to be working.

However, the exuberant excesses of unrestricted capitalism—that which produces fantastic wealth for a few—eventually causes serious problems for *all* of society. The monopolistic practices, overbuilding, questionable financing, and stock bubbles of the late 1800s eventually caused the Panic of 1893 with its bank failures and misery for the average American.

President Theodore Roosevelt and the Progressive Movement thus started reining in laissez-faire capitalism in the early 1900s by passing reforms to break up monopolies and protect American workers and consumers. Teddy Roosevelt was vilified by fellow Republican politicians for heresy against laissez-faire doctrine but he was adored by the American people.

A popular cartoon of the early 1900s depicts Roosevelt as a lion tamer snapping his whip at the monopolistic capitalist lions to bring them under control for the safety of the American public. The equivalent politicians today are, of course, Bernie Sanders and Elizabeth Warren.

The fact that these two advocates for ordinary Americans lack the popularity and even name-recognition that Roosevelt and the Progressives had a hundred years ago shows the power of the corporate media today. It also reflects the deterioration of community life and the political class consciousness that goes with it.

4. SCANDAL UPENDS THE MYTH

Unfortunately, people forget. Thus, laissez-faire capitalism had a resurgence with the Republican presidents of the 1920s—Harding, Coolidge, and Hoover. Their laissez-faire policies were reflected in unregulated stock market shenanigans—the gross, corrupt trading manipulations of the 1920s. The Roaring Twenties resulted. Laissez-faire seemed like the magical wand of a fairy that could produce wealth at will.

But there was a dark ending to the fairy tale. The cheery story of flappers and jazz had ominous foreshadowing that, for those with alert eyes and ears, would predict the climax of horror about to be sprung. F. Scott Fitzgerald captures the reality of the contradiction well in his classic *The Great Gatsby*, a novel that shows how ill-gotten wealth and the shallow life it engenders cannot bring happiness.

Fitzgerald's protagonist is Jay Gatsby, a mysteriously self-made man who spends lavishly trying to impress the blue bloods and to capture a woman's heart. Gatsby is killed in a case of mistaken identity by a man enraged over his wife's affair. Literature such as Fitzgerald's had as its backdrop the social and economic problems that occasionally bubbled up and which would soon boil over to become more manifest as reality then began to imitate the tragedy of art.

First, art first imitated life. As Fitzgerald was conceiving his story, President Harding died from a heart attack or stroke in the middle of the Teapot Dome scandal, which involved the government illegally turning over some of the country's natural resources to private interests. Like Gatsby, Harding was an affable, generous man who was not personally responsible for the scandal but who paid the ultimate price for it.

In later years, Interior Secretary James Watts and Vice President Dick Cheney would avoid such illegality with laws and regulations to allow such giveaways to private industry. The hypocrisy of neoliberalism is evident when welfare to the poor is routinely criticized but welfare to the rich is abetted.

The extensive turnover of public property to the rich also gives the lie to supposed laissez-faire neutrality and the neoliberal notion that the rich have created their wealth themselves. Many wealthy families today, for example can trace their wealth back to the massive government give-away of public lands to railroad barons during the 1800s.

The privatization of education and use of public funds to support charter and private schools are just contempo-rary, legal versions of the giveaways to private enterprise that characterized the Teapot Dome Scandal and the Robber Baron Era. One again, the roots of our current ills go way back. The rich continue to get giveaways while givebacks are demanded of the poor, the working class, and professionals.

Neoliberalism: A Western Fundamentalism

Religious fanatics often seek to rebuild ancient temples and churches with little regard for the feelings of other faiths presently on the land in question. Neoliberal fanaticism is similarly the attempt to rebuild the temple of classical capitalism that was supposedly damaged by heretical liberals and socialists. Like religious fanaticism, it also ignores the rights and feelings of people.

1. Coolidge's Temple

Following President Harding was Calvin Coolidge. President Coolidge showed the extent to which laissez-faire was nothing more than a *national, state-enforced religion* when he famously said:

> *The chief business of the American people is business…*
> *The man who builds a factory builds a* **temple**—
> *The man who works there* **worships** *there.*

Coolidge's declaration of official government philosophy reflects America changing from a rural, religious society to an urban, consumerist one by the mid-1920s. Before the advent of industrial capitalism, religion was the main leisure activity with which the people of the world occupied themselves. In supplanting religion, capitalism has become even more all-encompassing, dominating both work and leisure and pervading our consciousness in the way that religion once did.

Much of what we do for leisure today (e.g., shopping, going on cruises or to resorts, participating in activities that require an ever-growing list of specialized equipment) involves consumption that fuels the engine of capitalism.

Even when we spend little money during more passive leisure, the most popular activity here is observing consumerist lifestyles and listening to indoctrinating advertisements on television.

Such "activity" and the indoctrination that accompanies it impel us to buy something later—or even right then, using the smartphone. This is usually with money that we don't actually have and the ensuing debt forces us to work longer hours or even past retirement age. Even before the advent of debt, Mark Twain, who lived at the height of industrial capitalism, observed the following:

> ...[man] has always been a slave in one form or another, and has always held other slaves in bondage under him in one way or another. In our day he is always some man's slave for wages, and does that man's work... [xiv]

This, remember, is Mark Twain—that most American of writers—and not Karl Marx!

It was no accident that after the terror attacks of September 11, President Bush urged Americans to go to the mall and shop rather than to go to church and pray. It is similarly no surprise that Bush's brother, Jeb, said during the 2016 presidential campaign that Americans should work "longer hours." In an equivalent demand, the Islamic State requires Muslims under their control to perform their full five sessions of prayer. In line with Coolidge's dictum, *working and consuming are the pious acts that have now replaced praying as measures of fidelity to the values of the American society.*

Coolidge's comment explains part of the government's revulsion to strikes in capitalist society. Not only do strikes threaten the profits of the capitalist by reducing the output of the worker; they are actually a sacrilege committed against the sacred temple of the workplace. Just as religious attendance was enforced by the Puritans of colonial America and is similarly enforced by the Islamic State in Syria and Iraq, so must work attendance not be threatened in modern capitalist society.

Coolidge actually made his political name—and secured the eventual presidential nomination of his party—by breaking a police strike in Boston in 1919. If the business owner or manager is a *High Priest* in Coolidge's capitalism, then the union leader opposing management must be an *Anti-Christ*.

The scapegoating of today's teachers unions by political opportunists thus has a long antecedent history in the story of capitalism. This story of the historical demonization and persecution of unions is one that teachers, workers, and other professionals would do well to learn if they are serious about safeguarding their rights today.

2. Ideology Before People

During the Coolidge presidency, the economic expansion of the Roaring Twenties reached its height. It was partially fueled by that new innovation in capitalist consumerism— *debt*. As American workers became slaves to debt, they had to work to make their *payments*—the capitalist equivalent of religious tithes. The inescapability of debt was much

like that of original sin. To transcend both, a life of recti-
tude and regular penance was demanded; in one case praying, in the other *paying*.

**In all these ways, capitalism has thus become a reli-
gion in itself.** It is replete with the minute *absurdities of
the workplace* that are typical of the mind-boggling intru-
sions of fundamentalist religion. Such absurdities have
been brutally satirized by the brilliant comic strip *Dilbert*
in which professionals suffer the constant irritants of corporate mind control—again, the capitalist equivalent of
traditional religious mind control.

Whereas most religious people in the world today can
safely ignore the myriad detailed strictures and prohibi-
tions of their religion, *the corporate workplace is now the
institution that enforces absolute adherence to proper behavior.* This even extends to the worker's free time, as in
the monitoring of social media and the levying of sanctions for violations of company norms regarding off-duty
expression. In the same manner that Islamic State believes
errant Muslims disgrace Islam, so must one of Coolidge's
laboring "worshippers" never behave in a way that reflects
poorly on their employer's temple.

Although required adherence to extensive minutiae
can be as irritating at the office as in the church, the most
worrisome aspect of Coolidge's economic religion is the
same as that of other fundamentalist religions—*the insis-
tence on dogmatic, inviolable first principles.* And the most
dangerous of these is **the subordination of human interests to supposedly higher, absolute principles.**

In Coolidge's religion, shared by his fellow Republicans then and now, the most important principle, of course, was that of government non-intervention in the economy. The career of the next president, Herbert Hoover, would illustrate how the most decent of human natures could be hamstrung by such rigid orthodoxies of laissez-faire religion, a tragedy comparable to that of Fitzgerald's Gatsby.

3. THE HOOVER TRAGEDY

Hoover was a great humanitarian—a man who believed in acting *personally* on his Quaker ideals. During both World War One and World War Two, he organized important relief work for civilians in Europe that saved numerous lives. Franklin Roosevelt, who would later lambast Hoover's presidency, was so impressed by Hoover's humanitarianism in WWI that he actually wanted him to be president in 1920. Hoover would indeed get his turn in 1928.

The nation would find, however, that Hoover's personal humanitarianism would be rendered irrelevant as he faced problems that he *refused to comprehend*. Hoover's ideological rigidity prevented him from acting effectively to deal with unexpected economic disasters resulting from the shady economic practices that temporarily made the nation roar economically in 1920s. His belief in pure laissez-faire principles would similarly make him unable to deal with the nation's resultant growing social problems.

Just before the 1929 Crash on Wall Street, Hoover had predicted the imminent arrival of a *laissez-faire paradise* when he triumphantly declared, "We in America are nearer to the final triumph over poverty than ever before." Fervently believed, it was a message of *Good Tidings* that proponents of laissez-faire regularly herald when illegal and unwise laissez-faire manipulations build an overstimulated economy based on sand.

This promise of a free-market paradise is one that neoliberals still preach today—despite bountiful historical evidence to the contrary. History shows that laissez-faire prosperity has always been based on *temporary and unstable economic manipulations and irresponsibility*. It further reveals that such instability always later leads to actual *increases* in poverty.

As the *Messiah* whose *Second Coming*—i.e. reelection—would usher in the promised "triumph over poverty," Hoover absolutely believed that he had to follow the *sacred path* of limited government to bring it about. Hoover's confidence that the party would never end was the confidence that Jay Gatsby tried to project at *his* lavish parties.

However, in a case of life imitating art, Hoover's party came to an abrupt and tragic end as had Gatsby's. When the crash inevitably came in 1929 and was followed by the Great Depression, Hoover—following laissez-faire principles—basically waited for the economy to sort things out by itself.

When some citizens demanded relief in the meantime, Hoover protested that this would sap the initiative of Americans and that the latter could pull themselves up by their bootstraps. It is almost unbelievable how a man who could be so caring about victims of war could be so dismissive about the victims of the economy. *But such is the way of fundamentalist religion: the suffering of people is less important than adherence to absolutist principles.*

Again, we see such neoliberal fanaticism today when charter schools are supported even though many of them essentially steal the public's money and make little or no attempt to educate children. This current phenomenon of promoting the religion of privatized education at the expense of the American student and the American taxpayer is detailed in Chapter Ten, "Two Privatization Warnings."

4. THE MAN WHO SAVED CAPITALISM

Hoover lost his bid for re-election to his former admirer, Franklin Roosevelt of the Democratic Party. Roosevelt and other Western leaders started to rein in capitalism with social-democratic reforms in the 1930s and 1940s. The economy would be regulated more closely and welfare programs would be implemented to address the needs of those whom capitalism had tossed aside. The cost of this enlarged government and of relief for the poor would be borne by the rich through increased taxes.

These reforms introduced by Roosevelt and Truman in the United States and by the post-war governments of Western Europe led to an exponential growth in the professional class. Remember, this was an era when reformist governments in the West were trying to accommodate the interests of the non-capitalist classes so as not to endanger the entire capitalist system by ignoring discontent and thereby causing revolution.

In the 1950s, a child of working class parents could now go to college with a government subsidy (e.g., the GI Bill in the United States) and get a job in one of the new government agencies (federal or state). He or she could also become a teacher or work in private industry as a white collar professional rather than as a blue collar worker like dad.

Much private employment was actually made possible by government intervention in the economy. Government regulations introduced by Roosevelt prevented the capitalist economy from self-destructing as it had in 1929. Thus, parallel with the growth of the government and its professionals, was the increase in private sector professional jobs as the economy expanded under the protective structures of New Deal legislation.

The growth in all professional jobs continued into the 1970s as even the Republican Richard Nixon approved the creation of the Environmental Protection Agency and signed corresponding laws to protect the environment. The Democrat Jimmy Carter would later create the Departments of Energy and Education. Professionals in the government were helping to stabilize and manage the capitalist system that Roosevelt had saved. Education was supported and expanded and literacy grew.

5. YEARNING FOR THE GARDEN OF EDEN
Laissez-faire capitalists were vehemently opposed to the growth of the government for it meant restrictions on

businesses and the payment of taxes to fund government oversight. For them, the mantra "the business of America is business" meant that the interests of the nation were identical to that of its big businessmen. They believed that anything that purported to help the nation or its people at the expense of the freedom and bottom line of the businessman was destined both to fail and to hurt the country it was intended to help.

Laissez-faire thinkers believed that there really had been a capitalist Garden of Eden in America and Europe whose pure and efficient economies had been ruined by the government intervention of the Roosevelts in America, the Labor Party in Britain, and the various Socialist parties of continental Europe. Evil socialists and social democrats were like the biblical serpent responsible for man being driven out of his blissful capitalist home where he had lived in harmony with the divine principle of laissez-faire.

Like the religious Garden of Eden, however, the capitalist paradise has left no evidence that it ever existed. However, as the Guyanese proverb says, *the dog hangs his mouth where the soup drops*. Brilliant thinkers therefore promote the myth of a capitalist Garden of Eden because it benefits powerful economic interests in their societies.

One such revivalist laissez-faire thinker was Friedrich von Hayek of Austria. Hayek resurrected the discredited laissez-faire economic philosophy and repackaged it in what would later be called *neoliberalism*.

Hayek would influence Milton Freidman, basically becoming the John the Baptist of this refurbished laissez-faire religion. We will look at Freidman in more detail in Chapter Ten, "Two Privatization Warnings," particularly focusing on his support for a murderous neo-liberal fascism in Chile. Economic fundamentalism can be far more deadly than the religious kind—whether at home or exported abroad.

CHAPTER 7

---------- ✑ ----------

Bleeding the Patient Returns!

The Austerity Axe

BEHIND THE NOBLE-sounding ideals of neoliberal ideologues like Hayek and Freidman was the simple grasping
calculation of those for whom they shilled. The larger that
government became, the more it was able to control illegality in the business world. As the insightful comedian
George Carlin observed, powerful businessmen love small
government for the same reason that crooks like a small
police force.

Moreover it was taxes on corporations and the rich that
were funding such a larger government that more effectively
regulated business. For the rich, this was simply intolerable.
Why should they fund a larger government whose existence
was reining in their freewheeling activity? Government
would therefore have to be made smaller and the taxes to
fund government would have to be cut. Governments in
capitalist countries would have to spend less. They would
have to practice ***austerity***.

Neoliberalism is thus laissez-faire plus austerity. The original laissez-faire that lasted through the 1800s had no need

for austerity because government spending on the regulation of business and on relief for the poor did not exist. As we have seen, neoliberalism was a reaction to the twentieth century phenomena of government both regulating the illegal and dangerous activities of businesses and offering relief to those damaged by such activities.

The unbelievably wealthy beneficiaries of laissez-faire smoldered resentfully while the Progressives, Franklin Roosevelt, and European Socialists enacted reformist legislation. They saw the protective regulations and social spending of these governments as heresies against capitalism.

Progressive governments brought businesses under control, raised taxes on the rich, and engaged in Keynesian spending to stimulate the economy and help those adversely affected by the market. Franklin Roosevelt was horribly vilified as a result but said he would wear the hatred of the rich as a badge of honor. Roosevelt received numerous death threats. From the bile of such self-interested laissez-faire revulsion, neoliberal economic philosophy brewed as its potential beneficiaries bided their time.

Laissez-faire fundamentalists planned a counter-attack that bore fruit in the 1980s. From that time on, they would be called neoliberals. As indicated earlier, the problems caused for capitalism by a newly assertive "Third World" was another factor that led to this return to laissez faire in the West in the form of neoliberalism during that decade. As we have seen, an intrinsic part of this neoliberalism would be preaching the virtue of austerity in order to both reduce the taxes on the rich that funded social welfare and weaken the government agencies that monitored the abuses of businesses.

In the way that austerity is promoted, we find again *a religious element to neoliberalism*. In the early Christian church, asceticism was a noble virtue. Vows of poverty and self-denial were commonplace. Neoliberalism cynically exploits this Western tradition of Christian piety. It suggests that the demand for economic justice is somehow the sin of *"coveting thy neighbor's calf"* and therefore a damning example of greed.

In contrast, learning to make do with less while awaiting the *future blessings* of the market is a virtue that reflects good moral character. Just as practicing self-denying, Christian piety reaps the reward of heaven in the next life, so does quietly accepting neoliberal austerity eventually bring bliss. If we are just patient enough, we will one day reach the laissez-faire paradise of *bountiful milk and honey that trickles down to those who wait virtuously*.

Political neoliberalism began in the Anglo-American world, led by Ronald Reagan and Margaret Thatcher. The irony was that this reactionary movement was supported by many professionals who had forgotten their roots and their history.

Newly conservative professionals had forgotten that it was the social-democratic, "big-government" policies of US President Franklin Roosevelt, the British Labor Party, and the European Socialist parties that had enabled them to escape the drudgery and deprivation of the working-class lives of their parents.

T.S. Eliot would have indicated (based on his theme in *Murder in the Cathedral*), that they would pay for their deadly ignorance. Indeed they would. Austerity, with its savage budget cuts, would revive the old practice of bleeding—cutting the patient to death.

Poisoning Professionalism, Water, and Food

Many nights Tonya Cook made her rounds alone. She walked the halls of one of Florida's most-dangerous mental hospitals clutching her clipboard to her chest, trying not to think too much about the patients in her care. All of them were men. Many were schizophrenic, violent. One had chopped up a diabetic amputee and scattered him in parts through the woods of Dixie County.

One night in 2012, she walked the ward again, a single orderly watching over 27 men. Her nearest co-workers were upstairs, out of sight. They didn't see what a security camera captured—a patient holding a radio antenna fashioned to a jagged point. He calmly approached Cook as she sat looking over her notes. Then he swung.

Eyebrow. Lip. Temple. Eye socket.

As blood puddled on the floor, only the other mental patients at North Florida Evaluation and Treatment Center were close enough to help.

> *….years of neglect and $100 million in budget cuts
> have turned [Florida's state-funded mental hospitals]…
> into treacherous warehouses where violence is out of con-
> trol and patients can't get the care they need.*
>
> *…Four days after Cook had her face sewn up with
> 30 stitches, her boss asked if she could return to work.
> She tried. But every time she thought of going behind
> the locked doors of Building 12, her heart would race,
> and she froze. So Cook asked to remain in a medical
> records desk job that the hospital arranged for her.*
>
> *A year later, when she still refused to return to her
> old job, they fired her.* [xv]

Welcome to the nightmare world of professionalism that neoliberal budget cuts, Rick Scott, and Ronald Reagan created! As we shall see, neoliberalism was an insidious poison administered by a disarmingly genial potion maker who fed it to us with syrupy feel-good patriotism. The neoliberal potion was sweet but its effects on American professionals have been deadly.

1. AMERICAN WARS REPLACE AMERICAN RIGHTS

Ronald Reagan was elected in 1980. As an actor, he was basically a front-man for Wall Street and corporations like General Electric which needed a nice, friendly face to provide cover for their attacks on American workers and professionals. Reagan would exploit the patriotism and latent racism of those two classes to the disadvantage of workers and professionals themselves.

One of the labor groups supporting Reagan's campaign was the Professional Air Traffic Controllers Organization (PATCO) —a union of mostly white, well-paid professionals. Reagan had campaigned against "welfare queens" — those on welfare who supposedly buy Cadillacs and other luxuries with their welfare checks, paid for by the middle class. These attacks resonated with white middle-class professionals like the air controllers of PATCO.

Moreover, many of the PATCO air controllers were military veterans from working-class backgrounds. Even though the working class since the time of Franklin Roosevelt had been solidly Democratic for a generation, a Republican president had subsequently managed to woo segments away to the Republican Party.

In 1968 and 1972, Richard Nixon captured those segments of the working class who were prone to racism and resentment. These were southerners, evangelicals, and conservatives—those who felt that integration was going too far and that youth and women were getting out of hand.

In 1980, Ronald Reagan was similarly attractive to those members of the working class who felt it was time for the USA to overcome the "Vietnam Syndrome" (the reluctance to intervene abroad) and instead "kick some butt" once again to make up for the shame of having lost in Vietnam. This promise resounded well with the military veterans of PATCO who thus endorsed Reagan in the 1980 campaign.

A few months after Reagan took office in 1981, PATCO went on strike for better wages and working conditions. The problem was that as federal workers, these air traffic controllers could not legally strike. Reagan fired the strikers, destroying the union. This was the signal for private corporations to be similarly aggressive towards unions, both professional and working-class. It was the start of the process of real wages and benefits being cut, with workers and professionals slowly losing their standard of living.

Reagan, however, did give American blue and white-collar workers some compensation. In 1983, he invaded Grenada, an island in the Caribbean with an area of 133 square miles and a population of 90,000. This great victory was rousingly cheered by those Americans who had been stung by the defeat in Vietnam.

Reagan thus offered jingoistic patriotic fervor to substitute for the declining living conditions he was imposing on American workers and professionals. *We couldn't afford to retire and send our kids to college anymore, but at least we could kick butt abroad!*

Reagan's trick worked and he was elected by a landslide in 1984. The trick would be repeated by George Bush in 2003 as he plunged the nation into war with Iraq. Bush had lost the popular vote in 2000, but *he* also would decisively win in 2004 due to the war fever he similarly created. We can thus expect more wars in the future from embattled presidents.

2. STARVING THE BEAST!

From the time of Reagan, the size and power of the domestic, social-service part government (as opposed to its military and intelligence side) has been increasingly dwarfed by the size and power of corporations. The neoliberal policy has been to "starve the beast," i.e., to reduce taxes in order to shrink and render the government powerless in its ability to protect citizens from increasingly powerful corporations.

The shrinking of government has been presented to the public as a noble political philosophy designed to protect our freedoms from a powerful, overbearing government. In reality, the policy is designed to render government oversight ineffective. Without the funding for such oversight, our civil service professionals cannot protect us from the ravages of corporate depredations in an unbridled capitalism.

As a result of the neoliberal agenda to starve those who protect us, there are fewer and fewer professionals to do tasks that increase in number and complexity in our growing country and economy. These are the tasks that in essence make a society civilized, humane, and safe. As the article on mental health services that introduces this section shows, austerity budget cuts actually threaten the safety of the professionals and clients in that field.

Similarly, the actual *physical starving* of children under the care of Florida's understaffed and underfunded Department of Children and Families (discussed next in Chapter Eight "Killing Kids") is merely one of the more stark and barbaric results of this policy of *"starving the beast."*

Neoliberal austerity hurts professionals in practically all fields. There are fewer environmental inspectors because of cuts to the Environmental Protection Agency (EPA). There are fewer meat and food inspectors because of cuts to the Food and Drug Administration (FDA). Because of cuts to the Occupational Safety and Health Administration (OSHA), there are fewer inspectors to investigate workplace safety. And at a time of increasing US involvement in wars, cuts to the Veterans Administration (VA) have resulted in fewer counselors and doctors to help veterans.

These cuts from the neoliberal axe affect many more citizens than the professionals who lose their jobs. They also hurt both those who remain working in their professional fields and the citizens who depend on the expertise of those fields. The remaining professionals become overburdened with too many tasks, a problem compounded by the parallel cutting of their support staff. Such shortages result in important duties being hastily done or even ignored.

The examples are endless. Lack of security personnel results in the isolated professionals and patients at Florida's mental health hospitals getting savagely attacked. It results in patients experiencing neglect.

Likewise, ailing military veterans expire before receiving medical care. Even when treated, some die in the VA's overburdened hospital system. Similarly, because of staffing cuts, harried caseworkers at Departments of Children and Families throughout the nation are unable to ensure the safety of all of their wards, some of whom have died horrible deaths as a consequence.

Neoliberal austerity also hurts the general public in countless ways as fewer government professionals, e.g. environmental and food inspectors, are available to monitor the ever-increasing abuses of capitalist industry. Consequently, the people of Flint get poisoned by their governor's attempted privatization of the water supply.

Budget cuts similarly enable energy companies to contaminate our water supply with impunity through the highly dangerous and wasteful practice of fracking. These cuts also result in tainted food slipping by, poisoning and sometimes killing Americans. Austerity budgets allow mine owners to evade inspection, resulting in mine collapses that kill workers and traumatize communities.

Ruining the Economy

Neoliberals often proclaim that government bureaucracy stifles business and that cutting this bureaucracy stimulates economic activity. However, this is only true in the short term.

1. OVERFED GIANTS; STARVING DWARFS

While businesses that are regulated less can indeed engage in more activity and at a quicker pace, *such rash, unchecked activity always causes great economic problems in the long term.* These far-reaching and enduring problems far out-weigh any short-term stimulus to the specific businesses prompted by reduced regulation.

The various economic collapses such as the Panic of '93, the Great Depression, and the recent Great Recession were all *directly* caused by a lack of regulation. Their toll on people and society establish the damaging long-term effect of deregulation beyond any doubt.

Unregulated capitalism also *indirectly* leads to economic problems later. The lack of environmental and safety inspectors allowed British Petroleum (BP)to operate an unsafe oil rig in the Gulf of Mexico, resulting in its workers dying when the rig blew up. The resulting contamination of the Gulf of Mexico *destroyed hundreds of small Gulf businesses* that could not operate amidst the widespread pollution.

Hmm, helping the BP giant through deregulation that consequently kills hundreds of small businesses: what is the lesson here? It is this. Lack of oversight basically allows big businesses to immediately prosper while ***damaging our natural and economic habitat—the basis for all the future economic prospects of small businesses.***

Deregulation allows big businesses to illegally squeeze small businesses, putting them out of operation or making them ripe for takeovers. It allows big businesses to monopolize markets at the expense of consumers and the long-term interests of society. *Far from promoting free enterprise, the lack of regulations actually stifles it by empowering economic bullies!*

2. IF BASEBALL, WHY NOT THE ECONOMY?

Someone once compared the economy to a baseball game. There are apparently dozens of regulations that govern, for example, the size, material, and stitching of a baseball. And that is apart from how it is to be thrown, hit, or caught! Similarly, without referees a baseball game becomes chaos. In such a game, the strongest, the most brutal, and the most unethical win.

The job of professionals is to prevent such bloody, unfair, chaos—whether in baseball or the economy. *Neoliberal capitalists therefore dislike regulatory professionals for the same reason that cheaters in sports dislike referees.*

Let us switch sport metaphors with the New England Patriots in mind. Advocates of deregulation would prefer not to have any trained personnel around who could detect their deadly "Deflate-gate" manipulations that give them financial victory at the expense of later deflating the economy itself.

Whether you are a sports fan or not, go research how many regulations are in place for a particular sport to be successful rather than a chaotic failure. Then reflect on how infinitely more important the economy is. Draw your own conclusions.

3. MURDERERS ON THE BOARD

"Accidents" such as the British Petroleum oil spill are not mere unavoidable, unforeseen occurrences. They are the result of deliberate, cold-blooded calculations by corporations and the politicians who promote their agenda. Such calculations estimate the cost of environmental and worker safeguards versus the cost of the inevitable problems that arise when such safeguards are not implemented.

These sociopathic calculations put profit ahead of human life, the public welfare, and our habitat itself. They are the result of the neoliberal philosophy of shrinking government oversight in order to give freer rein for market forces to decide when human life is expendable.

4. REMEMBER GLASS-STEAGALL!

One of the neoliberal "reforms" started by Reagan and continued by both Bush presidents was the undoing of the regulations designed to prevent Wall Street from imploding as it had in 1929. Actually, our supposedly democratic process is so controlled by finance interests that even the Democrat Bill Clinton helped to destroy these protections.

The most important of the regulations on Wall Street was probably the Glass-Steagall Act, which was repealed with Clinton's support. Even Obama, voted into office in 2008 at the height of disgust with Wall Street, has not tried to reinstate this protective law because of his reliance on Wall Street for campaign funds.

The Glass-Steagall Act had been pushed through Congress by the Roosevelt administration in 1933, its very first year in power. It was specifically designed to prohibit certain investment behavior of the 1920s that had caused the crash of 1929. The law prevented the consumer banks used by average Americans from engaging in the risky financial ventures in which investment firms were speculating.

Glass-Steagall created an impenetrable firewall between consumer banks—mandated to be safe because they held the money of the average American—and investment banks, the playgrounds of irresponsible rich speculators. The reasoning behind the law was that if bankers wanted to gamble, they should do it with their own money or that of their rich clients rather than with the savings of American workers.

After 1933, Glass-Steagall and similar New Deal measures thus protected the ordinary American bank depositor by protecting local banks from the dark side of their much larger corporate owners.

The unraveling of Roosevelt's New Deal finance-sector protections through the neoliberal "reforms" starting with Reagan did indeed help big banks and Wall Street pursue bigger profits. However, this "freeing the market" eventually ended up sabotaging our economy.

The professionals at the Securities and Exchange Commission (SEC)—created by Roosevelt to monitor Wall Street—could no longer do their jobs of ensuring that the shady practices of the 1920s would not be repeated. The remaining SEC professionals who were not axed by budget cuts no longer had much of a legal mandate to ensure that Wall Street was behaving either ethically or responsibly.

It was as if the NFL had told referees to stop enforcing the rules governing the inflation of footballs.

Toxic Social Dumping

The result of deregulation, predicted by those not blinded by greed, was a repeat of 1929 and 1893—the stock market crash of 2008. This crash has gravely affected American workers and professionals, compounding the pressure felt since the neoliberal business consolidation of the 1980s. Understanding this consolidation will help us to better comprehend the effect of the 2008 crash on professionals.

1. CANNIBALISM OF THE GIANTS

Prior to the 1980s, wealthy investors had used their capital to open new, productive enterprises that actually created wealth. During that decade, however, they started to use capital merely to acquire other enterprises. The era of the merger, layoffs, and cuts began.

When a smaller company was acquired by a larger company that was listed on the stock market, the lives of the professionals from that smaller company changed dramatically. Their new CEO was responsible for producing larger and larger returns for stockholders. To increase profits, costs had to be cut. Professionals were therefore cut loose.

Many professionals lost the pensions for which they had worked for decades. The remaining ones had to do the tasks of those who were axed, resulting in more hectic schedules and longer hours. Guaranteed pensions were replaced with 401ks subject to the vagaries of the stock market. The professional merely became a more highly skilled worker.

2. THE DWARFS GRUB AROUND

The trend of pressuring professionals with more work and less compensation accelerated after the 2008 stock market crash. With some businesses failing, the pace of mergers quickened and layoffs increased. In another development, outsourcing replaced American and European professionals with those located in Asia. Working for much less, the latter could communicate with headquarters in the West through the wonders of modern digital communication.

For some professionals who remained employed at home, their whole employment status changed. Their employers turned them into *contracted* workers bereft of any benefits or rights. These professionals now had to grub around for contracts here and there in order to find enough hours of employment to put food on the table and purchase desperately needed benefits such as medical care.

3. GLADIATORS IN THE ARENA

For many American professionals, the work environment at the online retailer Amazon is fast becoming their own future. On August 15, 2015, *The New York Times*—in the honored muckraking tradition of Upton Sinclair—published an *expose* of the work conditions at Amazon under Jeff Bezos. The facts unearthed were stunning. Here are just a few as summarized by CNN:

> ...*Amazon relies on a system of anonymous evaluations....Because of yearly culling of low-performers, employees reportedly learn to make informal*

pacts to collectively leave negative critiques of certain coworkers...

One employee...after she had a child...arranged with her boss to come in at 7 a.m. and leave at 4:30 p.m. ...her coworkers criticized her... for leaving too soon, and she was eventually told by her boss that he couldn't defend her if her peers said she wasn't performing.

...employees were encouraged to debate and criticize coworkers in such a way that the work environment became hostile....a former book marketing employee said it was commonplace to see coworkers crying. "You walk out of a conference room and you'll see a grown man covering his face," he said. "Nearly every person I worked with, I saw cry at their desk."

Another employee...was berated for a half-hour about his shortcomings and given a scathing review... [when] he was promoted....lengthy conference calls on holidays, working at night and on weekends from home, and criticism for not being reachable on vacation were standard. [xvi]

Note the "culling of low performers," a social Darwinist concept reminiscent of the worst periods of the Industrial Revolution. Note also the primitive *Survivor*-type ganging up on the perceived weakest member of the group—encouraged by the employer.

Note finally the group criticism sessions reminiscent of Stalinist totalitarianism and China during Mao's Cultural Revolution. Indeed, two days after I wrote the preceding lines, Andre Spicer, a professor of organizational behavior at the City University of London, made precisely the same latter historical comparison in his article, "What Jeff Bezos Learned from Chairman Mao." [xvii]

Even when one has done a good enough job at Amazon to be promoted, one has to be brutally reminded of one's "faults" lest one think that his or her performance so far has been acceptable and one becomes complacent. Chronic anxiety thus becomes a job requirement.

These are the working conditions to which neoliberalism such as Amazon's seeks to return us. As Spicer points out, "like any vision of the future, it has striking similarities to the past" —*a horrible combination of the worst of both communism and capitalism.* This is what happens when the restraints on capitalism are removed. As so often in the past and in its current dealings with the developing countries of the Global South, unrestricted capitalism resorts to brutal methods to maximize profits.

Amazon is not an outlier. Other major American companies treat professionals in almost the same manner. Just two days after the New York Times published its *expose*, Emily Peck, the executive editor of Business and Technology for *Huffington Post*, wrote a very insightful article titled, "Amazon Only Perfected what American Culture Created." The title tells it all.

Peck quotes management professor Sydney Finkelstein of the Tuck Center for Leadership at Dartmouth whose assessment is this: Amazon is merely *"perfecting the American business model."* Peck notes that Amazon "pits workers against each other," with employees—to preserve their own jobs—needing to claim that their colleagues "perform badly."

Peck also points out the extent of the problem of white-collar, gladiatorial-type slavery. In other fields like finance, law, and consulting, none of what the Times revealed about Amazon was surprising. She also gives examples to show that such a cut-throat work environment also characterized Netflix and Microsoft until quite recently. Microsoft used to employ the "stack rankings" used to jettison supposedly low-performing employees. Peck also recalls the 2012 *expose* of that tech company by Kurt Eichenwald in *Vanity Fair*. It revealed a culture in which "managers huddle in a room debating the ratings of employees."

Robert Reich, former Secretary of Labor, reveals the hidden truth about the new, supposedly "family-friendly" policies for professionals at iconic companies. Reich points out that few professionals take advantage of these more liberal family-leave policies because of the cost (such leave is unpaid) and the need to stay on the professional treadmill for job security and advancement. Reich's article is appropriately titled, "America Is a Nation of Amazons." [xviii]

4. Dumping the Bodies

Peck describes the new type of driven and insecure American work environment in precisely Hobbesian terms: "nasty, brutish, and short." She points out that employees don't stay long at Amazon because of the "punishing work ethos." [xix] Instead of valuing employee longevity, managers at Amazon and many American businesses are happy to use and discard human lives.

Merciless business practices affect many more people than the abused workers themselves. John Newman, assistant professor of law at the University of Memphis, makes the connection from Amazon's employees to American society itself:

> ...*the real victims of Amazon's disregard for common social norms may not be the employees themselves, who at least stand a chance of enjoying those [professional] benefits. Where the costs or harms stemming from a transaction are imposed on third parties, economists agree that a "market failure" occurs.*
>
> *Many of the costs created when a company chooses to fully exercise its power over employees are borne by third parties. Destroying work-life balance harms more than just the one doing the work. It harms those who share the life. The fiancée who drove daily to an Amazon campus at 10 p.m. and begged his partner to come home. The family of the woman whose child was stillborn.*
>
> *By imposing these costs on third parties, Amazon creates (and profits from) a **market failure**, in much the same way as a factory dumping toxic chemicals into a nearby river.* [xx]

Many American businesses, following brutal neo-liberal practices, are thus engaged in what should be called *toxic social dumping*. Their troubled, damaged personnel are *dumped into the river of society* after they are used up and rendered *emotionally radioactive.* Though these professionals are decently rewarded monetarily, they are so physically and emotionally taxed after a few years that they either quit or are "culled" for being no longer as productive as they were in their prime.

The resultant social costs of physical ailments, mental health problems, road rage, divorces, and ignored children are borne by society. Schools bear part of this cost by having to minister to the neglected children of these professionals, one reason being that the children act out at school to at least gain attention somewhere.

Solidarity: The Best Defense

Fundamentalism and fanaticism kills. Sometimes they kill the body and sometimes they kill the spirit. We see this in the Middle East, where we have stirred up fanatic, fundamentalist religious forces with our invasions and interventions.

However, economic fundamentalism and fanaticism are just as deadly. Psychopaths are as attracted to the cutthroat business world as they are to religious war, politics, and the military. How do we defend ourselves from this insidious form of fanaticism?

Irrespective of whatever field they are in, psychopathic ideologues promote one-track policies based on one immutable guiding principle. With this principle—a cold, distant lodestar—as their sole source of reference, these ideologues dismiss the destructive consequences their actions have on humanity. Such suffering is merely the necessary penance society must pay for eventual salvation—whether religious, political, or economic.

Laissez-faire, neoliberalism, and austerity are dogmatic, fanatic beliefs in that heartless vein applied to the economy. "Economy" really refers to the most fundamental aspects of people's life—their conditions of work and their compensation. It refers to people's ability to raise their kids without crying each night after the young ones go to sleep. It involves people's actual physical survival. Ignoring this, neoliberalism has been blindly applied to humanity's very existence with the same disregard for human consequences as religious fundamentalism.

Neoliberalism has hacked and cut many to death around the world with its austerity budget cuts. *The neoliberal mantra that government is "spending too much" is merely a reincarnation of the blind belief of early doctors that the patient has "too much blood."* Neoliberalism has consequently bled its patient—society—to near death in many countries.

Neoliberalism has poisoned water in Michigan and deprived people in Bolivia of drinking water. The latter is an extremely illustrative story. In the Bolivian city of Cochabamba, the "water works" were sold to an American/European consortium in 1999. The company jacked up the price of water dramatically, beyond the ability of most residents to pay.

The foreign company also claimed rights to the entire water supply of the district—from the time the rain from the sky landed on the rooftops and on the earth! Thus, as a result of the privatization, *Bolivians could now be penalized for collecting water from their rain or streams.*

It was only through massive protests involving the sacrifice of lives that the people of Cochabamba were able get back control of their water. The movie *Even the Rain* retells this struggle against privatization well. *The Cochabamba example of solidarity and struggle is one that should inspire us.*

We desperately need such inspiration. In the West, apart from harming the general citizenry, neoliberalism is causing the slow death of professionalism. As we shall see in the next two chapters, it is this fanatic neoliberalism that is specifically destroying teacher professionalism in America and *physically* killing American kids.

CHAPTER 8

—— ✥ ——

Killing Kids

Death by A Thousand Cuts

*For every evil, every sacrilege, crime, wrong, oppression
and the axe's edge, indifference, exploitation—you, and
you, and you, must all be punished.*

T.S. ELIOT, MURDER IN THE CATHEDRAL

*Nubia Barahona was found on Valentine's Day in the
flatbed of a pest-control truck. She had been imprisoned
and starved, beaten and tortured, then doused in toxic
chemicals before her corpse was disposed of in a black
garbage bag.*

*The 10-year-old's death in 2011 was so grue-
some—and the Department of Children & Families'
role leading up to it so inept—that....the name Nubia
is a rallying cry to some, symbolizing everything that is
wrong with the DCF.* [xxi]

NUBIA BARAHONA MAY have died alone but she was not the only one. According to the *Miami Herald*, over a hundred children supposedly under the protection of Florida's Department of Children and Families (DCF) die violently *every year.* Here are a few others as summarized by the *Huffington Post* from an earlier, lengthy *Herald* investigation:

- Two-year old Ezra Raphael "whipped to death with a belt several months after being returned to his mother, a North Miami Beach prostitute and drug user."
- Three-year-old Michael McMullen "wrapped and tied in a blanket during a bizarre and cruel punishment. Child welfare workers had placed him in the home... despite 'red flag' reports the children were sleeping in animal crates, had bruises, were living in the presence of their abusive stepfather, and were possibly being drugged."
- Twelve-year-old Tamiyah Audain, "a disabled and autistic Lauderhill girl, lost half her body weight but remained in the care of an aunt before dying in the woman's roach-filled home of suspected starvation, her 50-pound body covered in sores including one so deep a bone was exposed....a *private agency paid by the state failed to complete a background check and paid little attention to the case* despite pleas for help from medical professionals and the aunt herself." [xxii]

America's youth are dying because the practice of bleeding the patient has been revived—not in medicine, but in economics. Rick Scott, the governor of Florida during these deaths, in effect signed the death warrant for these children with his ***austerity budget cuts***. As *Huffington Post* continues, "The cluster of deaths came after Scott said that budget cuts to DCF were necessary in order for him to grow jobs in Florida and the agency would have to *make do with less.*"

Even as kids were dying, Scott said of the DCF chief, "I think Secretary Wilkins is doing a very good job." Wilkins was indeed doing a fantastic job—of implementing Scott's budget cuts at the expense of the lives of his vulnerable young wards. Like the doctors of the 1600s, Wilkins and Scott ignore the effects of their cuts on those for whom they are supposed to care.

Rick Scott is one of the Tea Party Republicans for whom austerity is the *11*th *Commandment.* He was elected governor in 2010 by using over $70 million of his own money in his campaigns. It was actually money stolen from us that Scott was forced to spend to overcome the stigma of his involvement in Medicare fraud.

Scott had overseen the largest Medicare fraud ever at its time of occurrence, for which his company, Columbia/HCA was fined $1.7 billion. [xxiii] Having bilked the nation of billions, Scott was determined—like other Tea Party activists—to make the poor tighten their belts. The most vulnerable in the nation would have to make up the slack in the nation's coffers that Scott and his fellow business-men and financiers had created.

The effect of Scott's cuts to Florida's Department of Children and Families persist today. In 2015, on the day celebrating our independence as a nation, the *Miami Herald* reported the ongoing ordeal of a Florida girl sup-posedly under the protection of the DCF:

> *She had been starved and beaten, molested and forced to fight during her two years in foster homes and group care. As a runaway, she was trafficked into prostitution.*
>
> *And, just as her life appeared to be mending, the girl was raped by a driver in whose care she was entrusted by a* <u>*privately run*</u> *child welfare group...* [xxiv]

Note again the effect of privatizing government services. A pattern should be clear now. Private agencies, whether they are charter schools, jail operators, or child-care agen-cies, are notorious for hiring less qualified people or those of dubious background in order to cut costs so that the agency owners can reap a higher profit. Driven by the bot-tom line, they simply don't do the job as well as a public agency that hires qualified professionals on the basis of merit.

As I write this book, Governor Scott still swings the axe to the budget for the protection and care of children. During the first week of the 2015-2016 school year, the *Miami Herald* reported an attack on the Florida Children's

Medical Services. Medical professionals at the agency accused the administrators of purging six thousand kids from services and implementing a freeze on enrollment that forced "frail children to wait." [xxv]

Note again the connection between these budget cuts for kids' medical services and Scott's own illegal profit-making from Medicaid before becoming governor. Florida kids today are having to survive (and some are not!) without important medical services because their governor's company bilked the government of Medicaid funds. The guilty CEO then uses his ill-gotten gains to buy the gubernatorial election so that he can *make our kids pay for his sins.*

Rick Scott's tenure as CEO of Columbia/HCA and later as Florida governor really encapsulates the hypocrisy of neoliberalism and reveals this economic philosophy for what it really is: *high-sounding economic ideals that are used to mask the naked grasp for money and power.*

Scott's cuts to the DCF and to Children's Medical Services obviously *affect education and teaching.* What, for example, is the effect of these cuts on student learning? How much can students learn when they are experiencing such neglect and abuse?

Like other teachers in impoverished communities, I myself have taught students undergoing trauma or unresolved illness. I also teach children who are hungry throughout the day because the threshold for free breakfast and lunch is too low. The parents work at minimum wage jobs which barely cover the rent, transportation, and an amount of food that would qualify as war rations, but the income is "too much" to qualify for any type of aid. These victimized, ill, or hungry students are unable to concentrate in class or to study and do assignments.

Teachers are held accountable for the success of students victimized by neoliberalism and austerity. Such success has been sabotaged by ideologues like Governors Rick Scott and Rick Snyder who have implemented budget cuts that have devastated schools and communities. These fanatics promote noble-sounding political, economic, and educational ideals that merely enlarge their portfolios while jeopardizing our nation's future—the very health and education of our kids.

When T.S. Eliot spoke of the evil of the axe in *Murder In The Cathedral*, he had in mind the slaying in 1170 AD of Archbishop Thomas Beckett by Anglo-Norman knights carrying out the wish of King Henry II—an act symbolizing man's inhumanity to man. Today, in the West, the inhumanity is a little more subtle. The rulers of today, like Governor Rick Scott, merely have their underlings like Wilkins wield *budget* axes.

The axes of today are not being wielded in the name of the king's honor but rather in the name of a similar subservience to the upper class. That subservient philosophy is called neoliberalism and its axe-wielding henchman is austerity. The effect on innocents, however, is the same as that caused by the wanton swinging of the king's axe blades in the Middle Ages.

Kids for Cash: How Privatization Kills

Neoliberals cleverly attach privatization measures along with their budget-cutting initiatives, promising private sector efficiency that will supposedly keep budget costs low. This masks the real goal of using privatization to further enrich wealthy investors at public expense.

The "Kids for Cash" prison story of Wilkes-Barre in Luzerne County, Pennsylvania reveals the reality behind "efficiency" and "lower budget" promises. This story of the privatization of prisons is instructive about the real motives of those who similarly promote educational "choice" and propose privatizing schools. It is also a sad lesson about what the effects of privatization—as opposed to its promises—really are for the most vulnerable in our society, i.e., our young.

In Wilkes-Barre, Judges Mark Ciavarella and Michael Conahan used their authority to close the county juvenile detention center and replace it with a new one built by a private contractor and run by a private facility endearingly named PA Child Care. The new lockup cost $8 million but the private contractor leased it back to the county for $58 million. *The judges received kickbacks of millions of dollars for this privatization* and for ensuring a binding contract between the court and the private facility.

The judges then took kickbacks for each juvenile they sentenced to PA Child Care! (PA Child Care was paid for each day a prisoner spent in the facility.) To facilitate business for their private industry patrons, the judges pressured the parents of the accused juveniles to decline counsel for their kids. To rack up more "child care" clients for the private jailer, the judges then steamrolled the defendants and blazed through their judicial proceedings and deliberations, which often only lasted a few minutes. These venerated arbiters of the law gravely sent kids to jail for such heinous offenses as mocking an assistant principal on MySpace and walking around in a vacant building.

PA Child Care apparently loved caring for the children so much that it often extended their stay well past the sentences imposed! Or perhaps it was love of the daily payment for each prisoner that they got from the county. Jokes aside, such illegal extensions of jail sentences amounted to *kidnapping and slavery.* Neoliberal privatization has thus made it necessary for the "Land of the Free" to choose another nickname.

Wilkes-Barre's privatized justice victimized over 6,000 juveniles, with many kids' lives being ruined. It caused at least one death. *Edward Kenzakoski committed suicide after his experience with privatized law as a teenager.*

For each kid that was traumatized or killed by privatized law, there are dozens of family members, acquaintances, and friends who still carry the pain. This one example of privatized criminal justice in Wilkes-Barre therefore hurt tens of thousands of people.

Moreover, privatized law failed miserably to provide what it had promised—savings to the community. The highly inflated price of the prison, the needlessly incarcerated kids, and the illegally extended incarcerations all caused justice costs for Wilkes-Barre to rise greatly—and needlessly so. ***Neoliberalism not only damages us but also simply fails to deliver on its dreamy promises.***

Privatized justice also affects what happens during incarceration itself. As with privatized schools, the personnel operating private prisons are not as qualified or trained as those working in the public sphere. Paid less than public corrections officers, these private jailers compensate by amusing themselves with the prisoners in a manner reminiscent of a *Spartacus*-type movie featuring ancient jailer sadism.

Florida has been recently rocked with numerous scandals of private jailers entertaining themselves by abusing prisoners or sponsoring "fight clubs" and similar gladiatorial contests among the latter. Sadly, this has also been true of such jailers assigned to work with juveniles. *Such privatized jailer entertainment has ended up with some kids being killed.*[xxvi]

As opposed to Midas' gold touch, the profit motive virulently contaminates everything it touches. Privatized prisons are not the only for-profit facilities that have exploited and abused kids. The central goal of extracting maximum profit while paying the minimum for staff has resulted in kids being abused by such poorly qualified employees elsewhere.

In Florida, privatized child care for kids taken from abusive families has similarly resulted in *eleven-year old boys being incited to fight each other* to the point of requiring hospitalization and mental health treatment. Reviewing the case, the judge described *"cockfights"* provoked and cheered on by what he called *"stupid, inept" private staff* hired by the profit-making Children's Home Society of Florida. [xxvii] It is this type of privatization that neoliberal education "reformers" propose bringing to education.

Neoliberal capitalism resists spending adequately to educate kids properly in public schools. It prefers to spend that money on private jailers and other sadistic staff. Throughout the country, states are shifting funds for education into the coffers of those who build or operate prisons. In May of 2015, for example, Maryland spent $30 million for a new prison and then cut more than $12 million for Baltimore schools. [xxviii] Note that this was *after* the riots in Baltimore highlighted both the hopelessness of Baltimore kids and the problems of an overreaching criminal justice system!

Neoliberal politicians obviously value the interests of those who contribute to their political campaigns more than they do the interests of our youth. The effect of such warped priorities is predictably horrendous. In "Maryland Chooses Jail Over Schools for Baltimore Youths," Rebecca McCray makes the following astute observation:

> *The states making the <u>deepest cuts</u> to K-12 spending—Arizona, Alabama, and Oklahoma—are all among the 10 states with the highest incarceration rates.* [xxix]

As a historical note, the following is also no accident: ***the states which value prisons over students tend to be those***

of the former Confederacy or those of neighboring states settled by ex-Confederates or slave owners.

It is not a far stretch to move from keeping a large portion of your population enslaved on plantations to keeping them enslaved in prisons. Slave labor—then and now—is highly profitable to those using it. *Similarly, the laws that once prohibited teaching a slave to read or write are now replaced by the laws that cut the budgets for such instruction.*

The United States has the most prisoners in the world and the highest rate of incarceration. The privatization of prisons is the greatest cause of our becoming a jailer nation as prison operators contribute to the political campaigns of candidates who propose drastic laws (e.g. on drugs) and harsh sentencing.

The valuing of private profits over the education and very freedom of our people obviously explains neoliberalism's disregard for the future of our kids. *There are simply too many people who stand to profit more if our kids are not in school but rather in jail.*

The Death of College

Neoliberal capitalism is responsible for needlessly jailing our kids and then abusing and dehumanizing them in prison. It is also the reason why many kids are not in college in the first place.

The austerity fanatics have used their axes to slash funding for higher education. At the same time, neoliberal philosophy has infiltrated the administration of higher education, thoroughly infusing it with the goal of extracting the most from the consumer while enrichening top executives. University presidents and top administrators are now paid like private-sector CEOs (with many making over a million dollars a year) while tuition skyrockets to accommodate such outrageous salaries. Working-class and even many middle-class kids are simply priced out of college today.

Austerity also affects kids while they are in college by reducing the quality of their learning experience. Neoliberalism's elitist goal of widening the gap between management and labor has resulted in many low-paid, part-time adjunct instructors being hired to replace senior, tenured faculty. With no job security, adjuncts cannot challenge administrators about decisions that adversely affect students in the way that tenured faculty could. Remaining tenured faculty are themselves too intimidated by budget cutting to raise important concerns or else they are bought off with promises of future entry into the now-lucrative university management positions.

Worse, instruction quality declines as the numerous, harried adjunct instructors fail to replicate the unionized, tenured, more-qualified faculty. The adjuncts would be good instructors in a less exploitative situation. However, they are poorly paid and subjected to a neoliberal management policy that keeps them minimally employed so that they receive no benefits. Consequently, adjuncts have to cram in an overload of courses working at different colleges simply to survive. The typical workday finds them frantically shuttling from campus to campus to beat the class bell.

Through no fault of their own, adjuncts are used by college administrators to create a mass-produced educational product—with all of the problems that mass production generates. The college experience has therefore been turned into what is essentially a mental factory of the 19th Century. The college administrators are the factory owners who exploit low-wage mental labor to produce a deteriorating product for the consumer at an exorbitant price.

There are two neoliberal goals behind making public higher education more expensive. The first is to ensure that the military has a *steady flow of recruits* for the foreign wars that procure access to resources and markets abroad. Kids who can't afford to go to college and can't get a job often join the military. In return for denying them an education to broaden their minds and learn a productive career, neoliberal capitalism gives impressionable kids an indoctrination in jingoistic patriotism and training in the art of killing.

Those kids who wind up dead in the wars of empire thus join the other young victims who die in neoliberalism's prisons or from its budget cuts. Some of those who return alive but with untreated psychoses from the wars vent their untamable rages on those they encounter, leading to a deteriorating society for everyone. Even Sarah Palin acknowledged as much, referring to her veteran son as "hardened" by war after he was arrested for domestic abuse.

Neoliberal capitalism's second goal in raising the cost of attending public higher education is to *create business opportunities for private colleges*. The owners of these for-profits donate generously to politicians who then pass laws specifically targeted to help these questionable colleges at the expense of both the students they recruit and education standards.

As the cost of attending a public university approaches that of a for-profit college, many students will consider the latter instead since they are smaller and because these students have been subjected to extremely high-pressure recruitment. Across the country, there have been numerous cases of for-profit colleges unethically recruiting students who were either unsuitable or uncommitted to college work, but who were susceptible to false promises.

Led by educational entrepreneurs, private colleges take the students' loan money and then leave them without support at college, resulting in students dropping out. Those who do graduate often find that their degrees are worthless in the job market because the private programs are so shoddy. The kids are then stuck with astronomical student loan debt—not subject to being written off by bankruptcy. This life-long, spirit-crushing, enslaving debt is unpayable because the professional careers to which these innocent youths aspired are inaccessible.

The increasingly distressing phenomenon of for-profit colleges exploiting students and debasing the value of a college degree is well documented in an extensive *Miami Herald* series called "Higher-Ed Hustle." Two particular culprits— Fast Train and Dade Medical College—were so outrageously exploitative and inferior that they deserve to be discussed separately in Chapter Ten "Two Privatization Warnings" as specific warnings about the privatization of education.

CHAPTER 9

— ✑ —

The Death of Teacher Professionalism

A Bronx principal ordered her teachers to give up their desks…and had the furniture dumped at the curb— telling staff she doesn't want them sitting in class.

Donna Connelly [the principal]…also told teachers to empty their filing cabinets, which she then discarded. With class in session, teachers were told to push their desks and cabinets into the hallway. Custodians then hauled them outside and piled them like trash…across the street.

…"Figure it out," she snapped when staffers asked where to store their supplies, a source said…."All their stuff is in boxes, bags and on the radiators"…

…"Children watched as the furniture was cleared out," one said. "The kids saw their teachers upset about what was going on. It was dehumanizing."

…"How the f–k does someone with so little good sense become a principal?" [someone asked]. **"What kind of policy allows this to happen?"**… [xxx]

WHAT KIND OF policy, indeed! The answer, of course, is neoliberal "reform" management policy which seeks to eliminate the traditional democratic collegiality in education. This collegiality is the mutual professional respect that has existed in all professional fields. It involves decisions being made democratically based on discussion of the accepted body of knowledge that professionals in the particular field have studied. As neoliberal capitalism invades the professional world, it eliminates democratic, collegial relationships where decisions are made on the basis of science and reason.

In the place of cooperation based on knowledge, experience, and rationality, neoliberalism substitutes relationships where management imposes *diktats* that are often based on the bottom line of those with economic and political power. Neoliberal management philosophy is particularly contemptuous of the opinion and feelings of its underlings in education because the latter are mostly female. As a result, such diktats directed at teachers often assume the bizarre quality of Principal Connelly's purges.

When the incompetent doctors of Salem bled their patients to death in the 1600s, they blamed witches for those deaths, shifting the blame for their own malpractice onto innocent women. Today, neoliberal politicians bleed poor neighborhoods to death with their budget cuts, creating *failing communities*. When the dysfunctions in such failing communities lead to poor student achievement, these politician similarly shift the blame onto women. The culprit today is the American teacher. Principal Connelly is merely one of the many modern-day witch finders who scour the hovels to destroy such evil.

Purging Evil

Instead of promoting respected professionals to positions of authority in education so that they can make decisions collaboratively with well-qualified colleagues, neoliberal "reform" politicians insert outside *managers* over them. These education managers lack the background professional knowledge to make sound decisions in the field, basing their decisions on management *metrics*, statistics that hardly reflect reality in human service fields. They are loyal not to the ethical code of the profession but to their careers in the neoliberal managerial world.

Neoliberal managers move from one field to another, wreaking havoc in totally disparate professions but satisfying the cost-cutting directives of their superiors. Some of them, e.g. in Flint, poison the water supplies of cities. Then, like Darnell Earley, they move on to poison school systems. To prove themselves, these managers often behave in the brutish manner of Principal Connelly while ferreting out employees to axe. They are our equivalent of the medieval *witch-finder.* And just as the latter was handsomely rewarded for each innocent woman he put to the stake, so do today's education managers get fast track promotions for purging mostly female teachers.

Sexism therefore also contributes to the contempt for professionals in education since most teachers, for example, those at the Bronx school, are female. Even though Connelly is a woman herself, can you imagine the male staff at a police station being subjected to such extreme disrespect? The feelings of women—in this case, humiliation, gross inconvenience, and frustration—are just not considered important enough to take into consideration.

There is great symbolism in the principal dumping the desks in the trash. This furniture would have been gladly accepted by any charity. The principal, however, wanted to show teachers what she thought of their furniture, their equipment, their paperwork, their belongings, and ultimately what she thought about them. This is the sort of *cleansing operation* one carries out against witches. It is the sort of *purge* one carries out against *evil*.

The principal's point of disrupting instruction by having teachers push out the furniture during class time was similarly meant to simply show power and contempt. The confiscation itself was a naked display of force, reminiscent of the seizure of the property of accused witches in Salem in 1692.

Today, such confiscation is the type of brute force exerted against minorities by fascists when they seize power. From the 1930s to the present, we have all seen pictures of fascist groups contemptuously dumping the belongings of scapegoated groups into the street. The abusive, peremptory actions of Principal Connelly fit that pattern. They are the result of taking democracy out of education and the professionalism out of teaching.

Connelly's outrageous behavior at the Bronx school is just one example of how educational "reform" has been bringing the Amazon work culture to the American school. When "reformers" talk about reforming education, their first and most basic principle is to import the management techniques of private enterprise into education. Their reasoning is as follows: education in America is bad because the workers in education (i.e., the teachers) don't perform well enough. Therefore, to improve education, we must *bring the whip to the workers* (both teachers and students) in the same manner that private enterprise does. As with Salem, we must purge the evildoers.

As with the witches of yore, the purging is done through *tests.* Thus, importing capitalist management techniques into education has resulted in teachers and students being subjected to a testing regimen equivalent to the very "punishing work ethos" of Amazon. These Herculean labors of testing last the *entire* school year. Not surprisingly, this has had the same demoralizing effect on the American school that equivalent neoliberal practices have had at Amazon. How did we get to such a poisonous environment in what should be an uplifting field—the education of our young? We can find out if we just follow the money.

Money and Inquisitions

The eventual shutting out of investors from many "Third World" economies after WWII as these countries gained independence caused American financiers to look for new opportunities domestically. Education, with its annual 400 billion-dollar budget, looked attractive. For the profits to flow, however, education would have to lose its socialist-like nature of being under the purview of the government. It would have to be privatized.

But how would privatization be justified? It could only be justified by asserting that the underachievement of American students was due not to societal problems like poverty but rather to problems in the education system that resulted from that system being run by the government. The first task, then, for those wanting to invest in education was to document a problem of low student achievement.

Hence *testing*. And hence *sanctions* for those schools, predominantly in poor neighborhoods, that don't do well on tests. The ultimate sanction is the firing of the teachers and the privatization of the school. To avoid this, instead of teaching the curriculum to which they are assigned, teachers have to teach test-taking skills and spend numerous days doing the following test preparation: (1) prepping students on the specifics of the particular exam; (2) administering the exam; and (3) reviewing with students the results of the standardized test that often *has no bearing on the assigned curriculum.*

The teacher's rating and that of the school is dependent on the general standardized tests of English and Math. Thus, *all* subject areas have to become geared to those tests. This is especially true during "crunch time"—the critical period of the months before the test. The teachers at many schools, including mine under former principals, are specifically told to "drop the curriculum" and do test prep.

Apart from being drowned in test mania, teachers are subjected to absurdly minute strictures and disruptive classroom invasions designed to prove that it is teachers who are responsible for America's poor students not learning. Such policies, glaringly counterproductive to education, follow a neoliberal agenda that is quite logical. If education "reformers" can "prove" that public school teachers are deficient in their teaching, they can then make the case that the most deficient ones have to be dismissed and the schools privatized.

To meet the needs of this privatization agenda, teachers therefore have to use up an inordinate amount of space on their boards to attempt to satisfy the myriad visiting observers and officials who waft in and out of classrooms at will. These visitors engage students in conversations that disrupt their attention and often display the smug authority of the arrogant business executive, both in the classroom and in feedback conferences with the teacher. Let us look at each of these assaults to professionalism in turn.

First of all, in many school districts, teachers are required to *daily* post the following for *each* type of class they teach: *objective, state standards, essential question, agenda, lesson vocabulary, and learning scales for four different levels of student progress.* In addition, we also have to post the *common school-wide vocabulary and motivational school-wide quote.*

Most teachers teach two or three different subjects. Consequently, the amount of time and board space the configuration requirement takes up is unbelievable. This

Kafka-like absurdity obviously sabotages student learning. Many times I have had to struggle to find a little scrap of board space to write some important content information about history for students.

One of the ex-assistant principals at my school told our teachers while she was our supervisor that we should be testing students as to whether they had learned the different levels of the lesson's learning scales—not the content, mind you, but the *learning scales* about the content! Students themselves view teachers being mandated to post, discuss, teach, and test such information with amused incredulity.

The real purpose of the posting requirement is so that observers from the district can determine from a glance whether or not the teacher is "doing her job"—not her job of teaching but her job of obeying regulations! To satisfy the *observational needs* of such visitors, teachers are further mandated to post specific information in specific places, e.g., objectives on the front board and only on the left side of that front board. All of these minute regulations of *board configuration* make it easy to evaluate the teacher by simply looking at her whiteboard.

Whereas the inquisitors of Salem suspiciously examined raised black moles, in America today they critically scrutinize blank spots on white boards. Such scrutiny helps to satisfy the neoliberal agenda of determining which teachers should be sacked and which schools should be privatized.

Next come the visits, especially more frequent if the school is in a failing community beset by poverty and its attendant social problems. Teachers at various times during the day can be visited by their *principal, assistant principal, any assistant principal at the school (about three others), the reading coach, a subject area coach, their department chair, a visiting school board member, a district official, a corrective team from the district (three to five "curriculum experts" who may all enter together or at various times)* and so on.

In order to determine whether students are learning, official visitors meander around the classroom, talking to students at will. Generally, the less intelligent the visitor and the less experience he has as a teacher, the more he makes a preening, officious display of doing his job of supervising the teacher. These inquisitorial officials recall the judges of Massachusetts descending on Salem to determine who was bedeviling the children there.

Then come the conferences about the visits. Having been armed with a checklist of almost a hundred required behaviors to look for, the supervisors can *always find something defective about the lesson*. In their various conversations with students while wandering around the classroom, supervisors can always dredge up an offhand, spaced-out, mischievous, or truculent comment by an unmotivated student to "prove" that students are not learning, the lesson was therefore deficient, and the teacher is thus one of the culprits guilty of harming children.

Neoliberal educational "reform" actually *requires* supervisors to engage in such witch hunts. Supervisors are told that if a school, usually in a troubled, failing community, is doing poorly at its tests, it must be the fault of the teachers. The school is "failing" because the teachers were not supervised properly in the past to correct incompetent teaching. In order to improve the school, the supervisors must now correct the deficiencies of the teachers to document that the school is on the path to improvement.

Supervisors must thus use observed "deficiencies" to issue appropriate corrective evaluations that indicate "Needs Improvement," "Does Not Meet Expectations," etc. Teachers who receive such evaluations have to be put on a "Corrective Plan"—basically the educational equivalent of purgatory—under which teachers are *cleansed* of the evil of harming children. Such cleansing starts with visits by *additional witch finders* who scour the classroom to uncover *the hidden sorcery* that is still bedeviling the innocents. Then come the *exorcisms*—the conferences during which unrepentant teachers have their *sins* recited to them, are forced to *confess* their transgressions, and promise to begin the path of *redemption*.

Although *chastisement* is initially administered within the professional sphere, it can soon become public. The Los Angeles Times administered a *public flailing* to Rigoberto Ruelas Jr. akin to the more physical one the witches of Salem received. If such miscreants like the ones at Central Falls don't follow the path of *pedagogical righteousness* and the school continues to "fail," supervisors must use the documented "deficiencies" of the transgressors to end once and for all the power of these witches. In the Middle Ages, witches were put to the fire. Today, we are a little more humane; they are simply fired.

What the supervisors are not told, of course, is that they are merely pawns in the plans of neoliberal state politicians to privatize the school. Many supervisors unknowingly help to implement this hidden agenda because their own appetites have been whetted by their new powers over teachers. They help to perpetuate society's injustice with a pen. In this case, the pen writes the modern equivalents of Putnam's accusatory letters of charges in Salem. It writes the equivalents of the Papal Bulls of Excommunication. In other words, the pen of injustice writes the damning teacher evaluations and the deadly letters of dismissal.

All of this is only the tip of the neoliberal "reform" iceberg that is crushing teacher professionalism and sinking American education. The blows to teacher professionalism are many—too numerous to be all discussed here. They will be more fully explored in *The Teacher's Manifesto II*.

Superman vs. Democracy

One theme is becoming apparent now from the different strands at which we have been looking. This is the "reform" pattern of grasping for power. The inescapable conclusion is that education "reformers" desire dictatorial powers over education.

Ohio Governor John Kasich wants to be "King," if not over all of America, at least over education. The very title of the film *Waiting for Superman* shows the desire of "reformers" to similarly have super powers—the powers of a Superman who can overcome evildoers, i.e., those witches in education called teachers. Education "reform" ideologues crave extraordinary powers to reshape education over the sensible objections of students, parents, and teachers. Such powers can only be called dictatorial.

The fascist nature of the Superman desire can be found in the very etymology of the name. A controversial, classic German writer originated this idea of a human with extraordinary power. In 1883, Friedrich Nietzsche wrote about such an *Ubermensch* who would later be the inspiration for the iconic comic-book character, Superman. The central characteristic of this Ubermensch is the *will to power.*

The Nazis took Nietzsche's concept of the Ubermensch/Superman and transformed it to reflect their goal of dominating other human beings. When the German boxer Max Schmeling fought African-American Joe Louis in the 1930s, Hitler called Schmeling an *Aryan Superman.*

Domination is exactly what education "reformers" want to do. Their stated end goal may *sound* admirable, but the essential problem with fascism is precisely the belief that *the end justifies the means.* In fascism, the individual must sacrifice fundamental rights for the greater good of the state.

It is no accident that the greatest Nazi propaganda film was called *Triumph of the Will.* Education "reformers" similarly assert the need for the nation to have the *will* to exercise *power* in education, even if it means trampling on rights in the process. American education "reformers" have actually helped to create the fascism that Donald

Trump represents—the lust for a *Superman Savior* with the will and power to clean things up.

If the dictatorial label and fascist comparison seems overblown, consider the following. In highly distressed communities, where the schools are (surprise!) "failing," special appointees of the state called *Emergency Managers* have extremely broad emergency powers. These include the power to *revoke contracts* that have been democratically negotiated and approved by municipalities and the elected representatives of their teachers, i.e., their teachers unions.

Such revocation of contracts has never been proposed for police contracts in these self-same, perennially high-crime communities. We will explore such stark contrasts in treatment further in Chapter Eleven "Why Teachers and Not Cops?"

From Poisoning Water to Poisoning Schools

Education is only the beginning. Emergency managers have been appointed for entire cities, taking power away from the democratically elected mayors and city councils. The dictatorial emergency manager of the Detroit Public Schools made decisions for these schools similar to those which he made at his previous post. His earlier *Directorate* was as emergency manager for Flint, Michigan, totally in control of governance, including the water supply.

Like fascist dictators, emergency managers for school districts ignore the horrified cries of parents, teachers and students about imposed education "reform" in the same manner that as city managers they ignore the horrified cries of citizens about imposed water "reform." *Emergency managers—guided by inflexible, neoliberal capitalist gospel— move back and forth from poisoning our water to poisoning our schools.*

The highly selective attack on education and the democratic rights of teachers is therefore fast becoming an attack on the very rights of local communities. If we allow such attacks to continue, they will soon end up being an attack on American democracy itself. There is a reason why we study history. Those who would deny democratic rights have always pointed to an emergency caused by a threat from an evil source that supposedly requires the drastic curtailment of such rights.

Authoritarians abhor local democracy and always try to find ways to subvert it. Things turned out badly in the past when the citizens of this and other nations consented to the witch hunting of scapegoats, yearned for leaders who would do drastic things, and let such leaders exercise emergency powers. This threat to our democracy will thus be explored further in *The Teacher's Manifesto II.*

CHAPTER 10

— ✑ —

Two Privatization Warnings

THE SCAPEGOATING OF teachers stems from the desire of politicians in the pay of the charter school industry to discredit public education. It is an easy task.

The gross inequities of capitalism and neoliberal budget cuts have created angry, failing communities with social and psychological dysfunctions. In these failing communities, emotionally wounded students simply reject school. They disrupt school for the same reason that the children of Salem disrupted church services in 1692: to draw some degree of attention to their psychic pain.

The rejection of education by alienated students causes the abysmal performance of schools in failing communities. The schools are then blamed for that which the politicians and the unjust economic system have created. Once public education has been discredited by such witch hunts, damaged by austerity budget cuts, and rendered dysfunctional by torturous testing, it can be privatized as a source of further profit for neoliberal capitalists.

Education "reformers" point to laissez-faire theory to claim the supposed benefits of school privatization. *However, are their theoretical promises borne out by the actual results in states and nations where educational privatization has already been implemented?* Let us find out by examining two leaders in educational privatization—Chile and Florida.

Chile: Privatization under the Gun

One nation that has already fully undergone education "reform" is Chile. A generation ago, American neoliberals such as Milton Friedman enthusiastically supported using this country as a guinea pig for comprehensive neoliberal economic experiments, including in the field of education. Neoliberal ideas were rammed down the throats of a vulnerable population with a vengeance.

Everything that is taking place or being debated about education in America right now already took place in Chile forty years ago! Chile went through education "reform" that was supervised by Chileans who had studied under American neoliberals. Examining Chile should therefore give us a good idea as to whether education "reform" really is a good idea for America.

Milton Freidman, an economics professor at the University of Chicago, was the most famous proponent of neoliberal capitalism, including in education. A sudden change of government in the previously stable nation of Chile was a great opportunity for Freidman's disciples to experiment with a real economy in a real country. This political change, however, was a tragedy for the Chilean people, a tragedy that the adoption of Freidman's neoliberal policies would only compound—especially in education.

The original September 11 actually took place in Chile in 1973. Like ours, it also began with airplanes attacking a building. These were warplanes of the Chilean Air Force and their target was the presidential palace of the democratically elected President Salvador Allende. The warplanes were joined by tanks of the Chilean Army which shelled the building. When it was all over, Allende was dead and over 3,000 Chileans would be rounded up, tortured, and killed.

The CIA had helped to plan the coup. Kissinger himself had earlier said, "I don't see why we need to stand by and watch a country go communist because of *the irresponsibility of its own people.*" Allende's sin was that he was a socialist. Like our own Bernie Sanders, he was a democratic socialist who respected the electoral process.

Despite Allende's commitment to democracy, he was tarred with the feather of communism. (Remember, we do conduct witch-hunts abroad also!) The new dictator, General Augusto Pinochet, was welcomed in the United States and festooned with foreign aid, a far cry from the US economic sabotage against Allende which followed Nixon's directive to the CIA to "make the economy scream."

With the military junta controlling Chile, neoliberal capitalism would get a dry run in a foreign land that it could not get at home. Milton Freidman, the theoretician of radically laissez-faire neoliberalism, salivated at this prospect. In 1973, Freidman's neoliberalism—with its severe austerity budget cuts and jarring privatization—could not be implemented in the United States because of the democratic rights enjoyed by Americans. Citizens who can speak out, demonstrate, join unions, and vote can reverse economic policies that impoverish them. At that time, there were very few extreme neoliberal politicians in America because the Supreme Court was politically liberal and had not allowed corporations to choose who should be elected.

However, Freidman's extreme neoliberal policies could be implemented abroad if the dictatorship we implanted didn't have to worry about troublesome things like democracy, due process, and human rights. This was now the situation that we helped to create in Chile.

Pinochet turned to the Chicago Boys, Latin American economists who had studied Freidman's ideas at the University of Chicago. His military junta started implementing their neoliberal ideas in Chile. State enterprises were privatized—sold off for discount prices to wealthy conglomerates. Import restrictions were removed, hurting local businesses and their workers.

Poverty skyrocketed as unemployment grew by 1,000 percent, and wages were cut for those who still managed to hold a job. Shantytowns exploded in number and size, scarring the cities. The gap between the rich and the poor became a yawning chasm. The "Chilean Miracle" was an economic miracle for those at the top and a miracle of survival for those at the bottom who managed to survive both such misery and the abuse of human rights that destroyed opposition to the misery.

Pinochet also applied Freidman's neoliberal, free enterprise ideas to education. *A closer look at what Pinochet's regime did to Chilean education should be a warning to those influenced by the neoliberal propaganda that free enterprise in education will solve the problems of public education.*

The military government made two major changes to Chilean education. The first was to decentralize funding and reduce overall government funding of education. The second was to introduce market competition by privatizing much of the school system. These changes drastically remolded Chilean education along neoliberal "educational choice" lines with devastating effects for the average Chilean.

Schools in poorer districts now had to fund themselves for most of their needs. They obviously could not afford the higher level of local tax funding that wealthy communities could. This difference in local taxes, combined with the cuts in the national government's education spending, resulted in the deterioration of schools in poorer areas. Chilean education became increasingly stratified as the funding and quality gap between schools in poor and rich communities grew. As students in poor communities increasingly lost access to a quality public education, Chilean society itself became increasing stratified.

Despite being heralded as a solution to the government's destruction of impoverished public schools, *vouchers only make the problem worse!* The junta's introduction of vouchers led to an upsurge in the number of government-subsidized private schools. With local public schools declining in poorer communities because of reduced funding, the best students there—and only the best—were sucked out by private schools because of their high admission standards. However, the families of these transferring students had to come up with the cash to cover the rest of the private school tuition that exceeded the amount of the voucher.

The deterioration of the public schools became a cycle with schools initially declining because of reduced funding, then declining in composition as they lost their best students, and then further deteriorating as they lost the funding that accompanied those students (voucher money follows the students), and so on. For poorer families, this has continued to pose a cruel choice to this day. They either accept this deteriorating education or undergo the increasing financial pain of coughing up more and more money to supplement the vouchers simply to have a decent education for their kids. The latter choice became increasing impossible as the military junta savaged the working-class parents of these students with pay cuts and other economic blows.

The Chilean education system thus became even more stratified with the poor being stuck in abysmally under-funded government schools unable to afford anything else. Society itself also became even more stratified with poorer students to this day still experiencing difficulty passing the exams required to get a job or enter university. Make no mistake: *this is the hierarchical society that neoliberal proponents of "reform" and "educational choice" would create in America.*

Chile slowly started regaining its democracy in the 1990s. As it has done so, it has been rocked with *long and massive student demonstrations and strikes seeking to end the privatization of education and to restore public education.* Various Chilean governments have responded by slowly undoing the free-enterprise education "reforms" imposed by the dictatorship.

In America, education "reformers" always talk about **data**. Well, the most important question concerning data is this: *how did the previous experiment go?* In Chile, educational "choice" was a huge failure that the country is now seeking to undo! [xxxi] This failure deserves serious examination in America. After all, the education "reform" being imposed here is the same to which Chileans were subjected against their will, destroying their education system in the process. A good start for an examination of this Chilean education "reform" is the paper put out by the Council on Hemispheric Affairs called, "The Failings of Chile's Education System: Institutionalized Inequality and a Preference for the Affluent."

None of the neoliberal crimes that Pinochet and his military junta committed against Chilean students, Chilean education, and the Chilean people would have been possible if Chile had remained a democracy. First of all, it was legally impossible to organize, demonstrate, or campaign against the new economic, political, and social edicts being issued by the dictatorship. Even worse, these neoliberal policies were forcibly enforced against a backdrop of continuing disappearances, torture, and murder of those who opposed such injustice. Pinochet killed workers and professionals literally, *a dry run for the killing of labor and professionalism in America today.*

It is precisely because democracy is a threat to injustice that American neoliberal education "reformers" —our little Pinochets—attack democracy. *They seek to end American democracy in education and in aspects of local government itself.* To prevent neoliberal capitalists from fully turning us into another "*Chile 1973*," this erosion of American democracy is an issue we will explore more fully in *The Teacher's Manifesto II.*

Florida: We Fund Sluts and Scams!

> *Miami for-profit college operator Alejandro Amor had a 54-foot yacht, a $2 million waterfront home and his own private plane. Now he's headed to prison. On [November 24, 2015], a Miami federal jury convicted Amor of 12 counts of theft to government money…*
>
> *[Amor's college] Fast Train admitted…students who didn't have high school diplomas—using fraud to make the government think the students were eligible for financial aid. …Amor boosted enrollment by hiring former **strippers** as recruiters…*
>
> *Amor told one employee to…"hire the **sluttiest girls** he could find."* [xxxii]

In America, introducing free enterprise into education has been as disastrous as it has been in Chile. Florida, the state in which I teach, has been the leader in imposing this ideology of neoliberal capitalism on education. An examination of educational entrepreneurship in Florida reveals absurdly gross failures that belie the theoretical promises of educational "reform." The result, as in the Fast Train for-profit college described above, is the *thorough debasement* of education at all levels.

Florida promotes educational choice at both the K–12 and higher education levels. Educational free enterprise—with its dogmatic neoliberal philosophy and inexorable capitalist logic—operates in the same manner at both levels. Practices that have had a dry run at the college level are implemented at the K–12 level despite their demonstrated failures. A more detailed example of how introducing capitalism into education destroys both the education of America's young and the value of a diploma lies in the story of another for-profit enterprise, Dade Medical College (DMC) of Miami.

The owner of Dade Medical College, Ernesto Perez, was an *education entrepreneur* the sort of person who gives education "reformers" a thrill. Perez's complete training for his career in administering higher education was his 9th grade education and background as a rock musician. In that former career, he was jailed for six months for *"exposing his genitals to a 15-year-old fan."* [xxxiii] Other preparation for his career in private education included *aggravated battery*. [xxxiv]

Engaging in the sort of education entrepreneurship that neoliberal education "reformers" such as Jeb Bush promote, Perez paid himself over $400,000 a year as head of his school. He organized illegal campaign contributions to Florida state politicians. Like fly bait, the campaign contributions attracted politicians in droves to help Perez promote his private "school." According to the *Miami Herald*, these politicians "passed laws that helped Dade Medical, such as *weakening academic quality standards*." [xxxv] The students at Dade Medical College saw the results of such politically-connected education entrepreneurship for themselves:

> *Some Dade Medical students have complained that the school's health-career training was so poor that it put them at risk of hurting patients after they graduated.* [xxxvi]

Perez' private school simply lied to the students. It told them that the physical therapy program was accredited when it wasn't. Under investigation, the school collapsed in November 2015, with Perez closing his offices overnight without any notice and stranding students educationally. Over 2,000 students were left with ***"crippling debt and no career."***

Some of these students filed a complaint with Florida's Council for Independent Education (CIE) the state oversight group that monitors private colleges. The CIE dismissed the complaints. The *Herald* explains the reason:

> *The CIE, a regulatory agency whose board is dominated by representatives of the for-profit college industry,*

could provide no example of ever having disciplined a school because of a student complaint—despite fielding more than 2,200 complaints in the agency's 14-year history.

….Perez himself is a former CIE board member. [xxxvii]

Talk about the fox watching the henhouse! This complete lack of state oversight is no accident. It encourages the proliferation of scammers like Perez who can then donate some of their wealth ripped off from students to the campaigns of politicians.

The main fox, Ernesto Perez, had one last trick up his sleeve when he found himself under investigation by the *Miami Herald*. Perez hired a private investigator to dig up dirt on the intrepid reporter, Michal Vasquez, who unearthed the abuses against the swindled students. This is the sort of respect that neoliberal capitalists have for freedom of the press. It fits a pattern: buy off who you can (the politicians) and intimidate those who you cannot (the press).

Connections and money do work: the proposed punishment for Perez under a plea deal was a fine and one night in jail. This story—like many of Florida's educational free enterprise catastrophes—is in progress as I write this book. The latest update is that Perez will apparently receive *no jail time!*

The students at Dade Medical College were savvy enough to blame the politicians behind Perez:

> *Former Dade Medical student Jeremy Frierson [said]…."If you're helping out people that you know are screwing other people over, you're just as bad as them, and you should face criminal charges as well."* [xxxviii]

On that latter point, we should note that Perez had found a soul-mate in Florida governor, Rick Scott, the medical fraudster-turned-governor described earlier. He had actually been able to arrange a sit-down meeting with the governor who, like Perez, had avoided jail time for fraud.

Dade Medical College is far from having been the only outrageously fraudulent private college in Florida. Even before it broke the story of the abuses at that college, the *Miami Herald* ran an extensive series called "Higher-Ed Hustle" that exposed numerous types of gross abuses in various other for-profit colleges. Former recruiters for these colleges, speaking of their fraudulent, deceptive, and illegal practices, have said that they were "disgusted" with themselves and felt that they were "doing evil." Such practices included the following:

> *…deploying strippers as recruiters…lying about job placement rates and using high-pressure, boiler-room sales tactics, including a psychological technique called the "pain funnel," that can reduce a recruit to tears.* [xxxix]

Florida's for-profit colleges also deliberately recruited students who were either academically unprepared or unmotivated for college or who would never get a job in the recruited field because of a prior conviction. Recruiters also falsely told impoverished students that their Pell Grants would cover the entire cost of tuition, thereby leaving unsuspecting, vulnerable students with thousands of dollars in debt. Looking at these various abuses, we can see that Dade Medical College was thus merely operating in a well-established Florida tradition of laissez-faire educational entrepreneurship.

Florida's neoliberal politicians have been pushing the same entrepreneurship in K–12 education that they so successfully promoted in higher education. Florida's charter schools consequently have the same dismal history as their older siblings in higher education. Broward County School Superintendent Robert Runcie diplomatically noted the following:

> *The way the system is currently structured, it focuses on creating quantity and just letting as many players [as possible] come through the pipeline. What we really should be doing is controlling for quality.* [xl]

As with higher education, the more free-enterprise players that come through the pipeline, the more campaign contributions the politicians get—no matter how lousy these independent education "players" may be.

The flaws of Florida's K–12 charter schools have been thoroughly documented by major newspapers across the state. Thorough investigations have been conducted by, among others, the *Naples Daily News*, the *Miami Herald*, and the *South Florida Sun Sentinel*. The titles of the articles are telling: "Florida's Failed Charter Schools," "Unsupervised," and "Cashing In on Kids." These investigations have found *the same types of abuses* in Florida's K–12 charter schools that are characteristic of Florida's for-profit colleges. Specific examples will be discussed in depth in *The Teacher's Manifesto II* and can be accessed on the websites of these newspapers. For now, let us note the following general widespread abuses of the public's money:

1. TAKE THE MONEY AND RUN

Some charter schools start up merely to take state money. After receiving funds to educate kids, these charters close precipitously, leaving students stranded. The private operators don't return the money they were allocated and the state doesn't force them to do so.

The local school districts, though bereft of the funds allocated to the charters for the stranded students, nevertheless are left with the burden of now educating these vulnerable children abandoned by the education entrepreneurs.

2. THEFT

The operators of some charters engage in simple theft of government funds while in operation, crimes for which some have been jailed.

3. GRANDIOSE LIFESTYLE
A more subtle way that charter school operators misuse government money allocated to them is to appoint themselves as officials of the schools with hefty salaries and luxurious job perks such as luxury cars.

4. MANDATED LACK OF SUPERVISION
The neoliberal state politicians in Florida get substantial campaign contributions from charter school operators. In return, these state politicians pass laws *to prohibit school districts from monitoring charter schools to prevent abuses.*

5. REPEAT OFFENDERS
Charter schools operators who have repeatedly failed are allowed to start new educational enterprises, thereby hurting more students in new cycles of self-enrichening opportunism. They are allowed to pilfer more state money at the expense of local school districts where such funds would normally go.

In some cases, neoliberal state officials have overridden the denials of school districts and approved such highly questionable charter schools, ignoring the serious local doubts raised where the charters are proposed. When such approvals have resulted in failure, it is the local school districts who are the ones responsible for cleaning up after failed charters.

6. CRIMINALS APPROVED
Felons with convictions have been approved to start and operate charter schools in Florida several times.

7. EXTORTION OF STUDENTS AND PARENTS

Some charter schools illegally extort money from students and parents for various fees. This practice has included denying students the right to graduate unless money is paid.

8. BAIT AND SWITCH

When applying for approval from a school district, charter schools will present certain names for a governing board. However, after approval, when the district no longer has supervisory power over the charter, the operators replace the names on the governing board. The relatively respectable names approved by the district have been replaced by the type of hustlers described above.

7. STRIPPING STUDENTS OF EDUCATION

Unlike their for-profit college cousins, Florida's K–12 charter schools do not seem to actively seek out strippers as employees. However, many of their practices do strip students of a quality education. The various investigations by Florida's newspapers uncovered some revealing facts, including:

- Poorly qualified teachers
- Daily field trips because of lack of classrooms
- Classrooms that change daily, are dirty, and held in places not conducive to learning

The problems with Florida's charter schools are so numerous and wide-ranging that they can't all be specifically described here, but you can confirm them by following up on these citations. [xli] [xlii] [xliii] These abuses of public funds and America's youth are so outrageous that they will indeed be more closely examined, with particular examples illustrating them, in *The Teacher's Manifesto II*. For now, though, let us end this section on charter school corruption with one illustrative example of the unholy alliance of opportunistic politicians and education entrepreneurs. Such alliances inevitably engender the corruption for which we all pay.

In Opa-Locka, Florida, the politician-entrepreneur alliance in charter school education is actually cemented in a marriage. The mayor of the city is Myra Taylor and her husband, John Taylor, is the bishop of a local Protestant church. Using their political and religious influence, they founded a charter school, Vankara Educational Center. The *Miami Herald* reports on the unsurprising result of such an alliance:

> *The couple was caught diverting tens of thousands of dollars...from a charter school founded by the mayor to benefit the family, including payments for two Mercedes-Benzes, and a host of other expenses that led to tax-evasion convictions.* [xliv]

Of course, as we have seen earlier, the politician and the education entrepreneur do not have to be married to engage in such corruption. In the other cases, they are simply married to the love of the gullible public's money.

In the Vankara charter school scandal, we see *the precise reason why some leaders in the African-American community advocate for charter schools.* With charters being under local control and not subject to the strict oversight of public schools, some corrupt religious and political leaders exploit the respect of their faithful congregations and betray the trust of their vulnerable communities.

Influential community leaders seize the opportunity to enrich themselves through charter schools under the cover of privatized black "community empowerment." White neoliberal politicians willingly permit such *local* embezzlement in order to promote their own agenda of more large-scale and widespread charter school *industry* corruption.

Privatization vs. Democracy

The story of Florida's for-profit colleges and charter-schools is the story of the damage wreaked by the unregulated privatized education that neoliberal capitalists promote. As we have seen, this education entrepreneurship ruins education at all levels.

These rip-offs derive from the neoliberal capitalist philosophy of not regulating businesses even when they seek to gain a profit by any means. The defrauding of student citizens and of taxpayers (through the misuse of government grants or charter school allocations) derives from capitalist control of our democracy. Such control places the interests of those who donate to politicians above the interests of the citizens for whom our representatives are supposed to look out.

The story of the destruction of American education can be summarized as follows.

First, politicians fill their pockets with legalized bribery from charter-school special interests. These bribes are then used in expensive propaganda campaign advertisements to soften the minds of the public to prepare them for the budget cuts and privatization that will follow the elections.

During the political campaigns, the corporate media puts out biased editorial analyses—as opposed to the honest news investigations conducted by reporters—that continue the work of the political advertisements. These opinions tout the advantages of competition and private enterprise while lambasting public education. After being elected, politicians sabotage public education with budget cuts. Then they weaken educational standards and the accountability over private education in order to help education entrepreneurs. These education vultures then voraciously move in to feed on the public trough with little accountability.

In Chile, it took a violent military coup and repression for education to be privatized. In America, all it takes is brainwashing about the myth of the superiority of laissez-faire and the private sector. Thirty years of dictatorship and neoliberal governments failed to convince Chileans of the superiority of such privatization.

In contrast, many Americans are absolutely convinced—despite abundant evidence to the contrary—of the superiority of privatized education. They fondly hold this illusion to the detriment of their children and their country. As Steven Biko, the South African martyr killed by the apartheid government said, "The greatest weapon in the hand of the oppressor is the mind of the oppressed."

The legalized bribery that dominates our elections with expensive campaign advertisements is part of what controls our minds. This bribery of campaign contributions also creates glaring discrepancies in how neoliberal politicians treat private education as opposed to public education. These politicians allow private K–12 Florida schools to avoid the grueling battery of standardized tests that they foist on public K–12 schools.

The point of treating private schools indulgently is quite clear: to get students and parents fed up with testing to switch to private schools. It works, even in cases where such a switch is embarrassing to the parent. The following revealing article shows how neoliberal state politicians create business for their private school donors:

> *Broward School Board member Abby Freedman has withdrawn her son from the public school system she helps to oversee, deciding he would be better off in private school. Freedman…now pays $23,900 to send her 12-year old son…to…Pine Crest School…*

> *Her concern isn't with her son's former [public]*
> *school...or the county school district. Instead, she said*
> *she's fed up with state-mandated testing....*
>
> *Pine Crest...has been ranked by the Washington*
> *Post as one of the best schools in the country...But what*
> *most impressed Freedman is that instructors teach with-*
> *out constantly drilling kids for high-stakes tests...* [xlv]

Note that the private school Pine Crest is nationally ranked without engaging in "drill and kill" test preparation. Note also that the only reason Abby Freedman's decision made the news is because she is a School Board member. Nationally, thousands of parents quietly make this decision every year for the same reason of onerous testing.

The attitude of neoliberal politicians to school oversight also reveals a similarly hypocritical double-standard in the treatment of private/charter schools versus public schools. The *Herald* article on Dade Medical College reported that one lawmaker who wanted to regulate for-profit colleges to eliminate their abuses "met resistance from some lawmakers who don't want to regulate for-profits." These are the same lawmakers, however, who demand strict oversight, accountability, and impossible expectations from public schools. Similarly, state lawmakers prevent district officials from having meaningful oversight over charter schools.

The discrepancy in the accountability for private/charter schools versus public schools derives from the baser motives behind the high-sounding neoliberal philosophy. This philosophy promotes unregulated private enterprise as an unquestioned *quasi-religious* first principle that leads to efficiency and quality. It should be quite obvious from the discussion in the previous sections that this is a false prophecy.

However, abuses in free-enterprise education are ignored because education entrepreneurs like Perez of Miami Dade College have bought off the politicians. In a glaring contrast, public education is harassed continuously to render it dysfunctional so that students succumb to the snake-oil pitches of the education hustlers of charter schools and private colleges. All that privatization does in fill the pockets of hustlers like Perez, leaving students without an education and without a future.

We can also learn a lesson about educational entrepreneurship from the sad experience of the privatization shoved down the throats of Chileans. *Neoliberal capitalism's first experiment—that of Chile—required a suppression of freedom in order to be implemented.* Such suppression was absolutely essential because of neoliberalism's adverse effect on the majority of the Chilean people. With this in mind, we can now fully understand *the Chilean-ization of American education.*

In Chile, the loss of democracy in society and education came abruptly, starting on September 11, 1973. In America, it has been a slower process, with creeping suppression of the rights of students, teachers, and communities as neoliberal "reform" advocates implement their policies in American education. Because our loss of democratic rights in education has been more gradual than in Chile, it has not been as easily apparent. However, this erosion of democracy has been just as real.

As young citizens, students have the right to a free, meaningful, and well-rounded education. This is a fundamental democratic right. However, just as this right was revoked in Chile under Pinochet's dictatorship, so is it being whittled away in America. As in Chile, the funding for public education is being cut in many states and in others it is simply not keeping pace with inflation.

Furthermore, just as happened in Chile, an increasing percentage of education funding is now being bestowed on charter schools, both profit and "non-profit." Many of the supposedly "non-profit" charter schools are only that in name; their trustees are also school officials who earn hefty salaries and have extensive expense accounts, courtesy of your tax dollar and mine. The democratic funding of education is thus being subverted as public funds are diverted for private, non-educational ends.

Apart from charter school allocations, other parts of the education budget are being diverted as voucher money to private schools. As in Chile, the families of students who attend these schools have to make up the difference between tuition costs and the amount allocated for each voucher. These families would not have to bear such a cost if enough funds were spent on improving the educational experience for students in the public schools in the first place.

If the proponents of neoliberal capitalism have their way, we will eventually end up with a Chilean-type system of education with socially and racially segregated schools. Because of budget cuts and onerous testing that forces the middle class out, public schools will have degenerated to the point where they are used mostly by the alienated, hopeless poor. In these failing communities, charter schools will be attended by the motivated poor to avoid the disruptive children of the hopeless poor who act out their frustrations in the public classroom, disrupting education in the process.

At the middle, a new crop of private schools will join religious schools. Here the middle class will have to supplement the government voucher with tuition money of their own in order to avoid the chaos that testing and budget cuts have wreaked in public schools.

At the upper middle level, some charter schools will open in well-to-do Caucasian neighborhoods that are not large enough to have their own public school. The parents here will start charter schools to prevent their kids from being bused to public schools in adjoining larger poor and minority neighborhoods that are rough. This has actually already started, e.g. on some of the islands off the west coast of Florida.

It's not that these white parents avoiding poor and minority neighborhoods are racist; it just that the safety of their kids comes first. The separated charter schools attended by these upper-middle class families will become "good" schools precisely because their clientele enjoy the privileges conducive to maximally benefitting from education. Moreover, the privileged, white students there will not be disrupted by angry students—black and white—alienated by their poverty.

At the very top will be traditional elitist private schools, unaffected by all of this and attended by the children of the neoliberal politicians and education entrepreneurs who have created this educational dystopia. Also attending these schools will be the children of America's police chiefs. The latter are now part of the elite that enforces the privileges of the rest. Like privatization, police elitism is inimical to democracy. The double-standard in the treatment of police and teachers is the subject of the next chapter.

CHAPTER 11

— ✐ —

Why Teachers and Not Cops?

A man works from sun-up to sundown,
But a woman's work is never done.

Boys will be boys!

ENGLISH FOLK SAYINGS

Failing Police Precincts? No Criminal Left Behind?

WHY ARE TEACHERS treated differently than cops? One basic answer is simple: *sexism!* The teaching profession consists mostly of females while all law enforcement professions mostly consist of males.

Moreover, the nature of both professions reflects the stereotypical roles assigned to each gender. Teaching is one of the *helping* professions associated with the role of nurturing traditionally relegated to women. Law enforcement, on the contrary, is one of the *armed*, protective professions traditionally occupied by men. These two differences of (1) *gender demography* and (2) *gender roles* result in society having vastly different expectations of work performance for these professions and vastly different attitudes towards teachers and cops.

Police brutality and the unjustified killing of civilians, particularly minorities, have finally broken into the consciousness of the American media and public. Yet this mistreatment of civilians is nothing new. The long toleration of such abuse reflects how misbehavior by male officials, even when it is a danger to the public, is tolerated.

More importantly, there are numerous other types of police misconduct and the shirking of duties that still have not attracted any serious attention from media commentators, politicians, or the public. Some are just plain laughable, but other infractions are just as bad as the mistreatment of civilians.

As we shall see, *such other gross misbehavior and non-performance of duty by cops has also long been tolerated,* again a notable contrast to the longstanding hounding of teachers. As you read about the stories of errant cops, just imagine what would have been the reaction had it been teachers.

Police Failures

The following headline-making events reflect just a mere fraction of a long and tortured history, one that goes way beyond the obvious and now-acknowledged cases of police brutality and unwarranted killings. From this painful history, taken mostly from local cases detailed in my hometown newspaper, the *Miami Herald*, we can see that there is a long-term problem of *ignoring the multiplicity of bad behavior* in the male profession of law enforcement.

Some of the examples below are so unbelievable that they warrant extensive quotations from the original news articles. The titles of the news articles are themselves revealing in their pithy summations of these wide-ranging police problems which, unlike police brutality, have *not* become an issue despite their seriousness:

1. Chicago, Illinois, 2015: *But the Car Seats Are So Soft!*

According to the FBI, crime went up in 2015. How does the FBI explain this? Nope, it's not because of too many donut runs. Nor is it due to Keystone-cops type incompetence. When police don't achieve what is expected of them, stereotypical insults are thankfully not hurled at them as they are at teachers.

Instead, the FBI Director James Comey points to the *real reasons* for declining police success: "availability of cheaper heroin, guns getting into the wrong hands for wrongdoing, and street gangs becoming smaller and more territorial." [xlvi] These are certainly valid explanations, but what Comey says next is interesting.

Comey goes beyond legitimate explanations for police failure to control crime by making an extraordinary claim. In a *Huffington Post* article titled "FBI Director Blames Crime on Police Misconduct Videos," Comey is quoted as blaming "ever-present cellphone cameras and viral videos" for the rise in crime, claiming that police are unwilling to do their jobs effectively while being filmed. As evidence, Comey points to cops who complained about young people taunting them with cell-phone cameras and who confided to him about their reactions to such taunts, "'We feel like we're under siege and we don't feel much like getting out of our cars.'"

"We don't feel much like getting out of our cars!" Comey made absolutely no critical comment about this dereliction of duty by cops who prefer to stay seated in the comfort of their air-conditioned cars rather than pound the pavement. Instead, he unquestioningly accepts the police complaint about being filmed as a legitimate reason for some police shirking their duties and the consequential rise in crime.

2. MIAMI, FLORIDA, 2015: *NOW WE KNOW HOW "COPPING A FEEL!" ORIGINATED!*

Want to know what it takes to be Chief of Police? Meet Jesus Aguiar. Jesus' career goal is to "reach the top." His top boss, Police Chief Rene Landa, describes him as "most competent and professional." His supervisor, Major Louis Fata, concurs that Aguiar could even become police chief someday. After all, there are only a few minor blemishes on his record involving inconsequential persons:

> *Lt. Jesus Aguiar has shoved his hand down the slack of a female subordinate and allegedly manhandled two women in a bar while "drunk and slurry," then*

repeatedly slugged a bystander who came to their aid, according to internal files at the South Miami Police Department.

The boss of an estranged girlfriend said he showed up at their office in uniform, handcuffed the girlfriend and pepper-sprayed her. He has admitted to using his police computer to look up the address of a woman he met at a bar, whose front door he then pounded on at 3 in the morning, startling her mother-in-law.

…a former Miami police chief…recommended that he be fired or at least demoted. Neither occurred.

Dismissing repeated patterns of misbehavior is not uncommon, especially in smaller departments said [Pat] Franklin [an internal affairs investigator]. [xlvii]

Aguiar's qualifications for his present job include dropping out of high school and earning a felony arrest. The female subordinate who complained about the sexual molestation in the above quote also described repeated harassment for which Aguiar had to apologize.

Note the tolerance for repeated misbehavior, with Aguiar achieving the rank of detective in half the time it usually takes. Note also the lack of concern that Aguiar's supervisors have about his attitude to women, with his complaints "disproportionately [involving] women."

When uniformed men can abuse and harass female citizens with impunity, are we moving away from democracy towards an authoritarian state? Is there a connection between society tolerating this physical abuse of women by uniformed men and it tolerating the emotional *abuse* directed against the mostly female profession of teaching?

3. <u>Miami, Florida, 2015</u>: *Laundering Promotes Cleanliness. No?*

Free-market "reformers" complain about the size of school budgets, teachers' salaries, and the union "bosses" representing teachers. Yet, they never say a word when the police abuse their budgets and police chiefs act like mobsters. Michael Sallah, a *Miami Herald* investigative reporter, describes the following case that is so outrageous that the silence of these neoliberals concerning it reveals their hypocrisy:

> *Just days after his undercover police flouted state law by using drug cash to pay their informants, Bal Harbour Chief Tom Hunker hosted dozens of police chiefs at the elegant Sea View Hotel, complete with dinner, an open bar and a $500-a-night cigar roller.*
>
> *As the staff served lamb chop appetizers under a white canopy, Hunker's men were about to secretly move drug money into a bank in Panama in direct violation of U.S. policies that ban illicit dollars from being sent offshore.*
>
> *....The charismatic chief showered public officials with dinners and gifts—including gold-plated police badges and expensive cigars—as the task force he created broke nearly every provision of undercover sting operations while* **laundering millions for drug organizations**... [xlviii]

According to the *Herald* article, Hunker was the "most important person in the government of the city," with elected politicians such as Patricia Cohen, Bal Harbour deputy mayor, commenting, "You could see how powerful he was getting."

Nationally, no politician commented about the threat posed to our democracy by the chief of an armed service illegally wielding such great political and economic power.

4. MIAMI, FLORIDA, 2014: *SO THAT'S WHY IT'S CALLED A* **FRATERNAL** *ORDER!*

Remember the condemnation of the Central Falls teachers union which committed the crime of asking for extra pay as compensation for longer hours and extra duties? Compare the actions of such educator unions with that of the following police union as described by *Miami Herald* columnist, Fred Grimm. This columnist is so insightful about the disparity in the treatment of police unions versus the treatment of other public service unions that he starts with such a comparison, involving a hypothetical janitors union:

> *Imagine if it had been, say, a mob of angry janitors, packing heat, who had besieged City Hall last month, shouting, banging on glass partitions, disrupting the city commission meeting, sending commissioners fleeing from the dais, scaring the hell out of staffers.*
>
> *You know what would have happened. Police would have been summoned. The janitors would have*

been tasered, arrested, cuffed, hauled to jail. Because, as Police Chief Manuel Orosa has noted, "disruption of a governmental official meeting is a prosecutable crime."

Except these weren't janitors flouting the law, but an unruly mob of cops, come to harass city officials who've resisted union's contract demands. Also, for good measure, they want Orosa fired. Javier Ortiz, president of the Fraternal Order of Police, called the disorderly demonstration, an "exercise our First Amendment rights."

It looked more like **intimidation** [xlix]

There you have it! Cops can actually *physically intimidate the public and elected officials* in order to get a better contract and to have the police chief fired. They face *no consequences.* All that happens is that they get a warning not to do it again from their police chief.

Neither President Obama nor any other national politician has commented on this phenomenon that is so dangerous to our democracy—that of an armed service threatening the government! Teachers unions, however, are lambasted for merely speaking and writing about the interests of teachers.

The discrepancy is stark indeed: the *outrageous and illegal* behavior of cops is tolerated while the *legitimate advocacy* of teachers is condemned! This discrepancy is rooted in the fact that most cops are men and most teachers are women. Men get to speak up. Men get to threaten. Men even get to threaten with guns! Women have to remain silent. Women, as with the Central Falls teachers, have to passively accept the extra duties assigned to them.

5. Rio Arriba, New Mexico, 2014: *How Low Can He Go?*

Neoliberal "reformers" continually complain that it is hard to get rid of bad teachers. Yet, outside of the flagrant cases of police brutality and killings, we don't hear much commentary about police misconduct and getting rid of bad cops like Lt. Aguiar mentioned in example #2 above.

When concerns are voiced, those who criticize the specific misbehaving policeman are quick to praise other police. Consider this case of road rage and corruption in blue that gets passed off an isolated incident:

> *…jurors convicted [Rio Arriba County Sheriff Thomas Rodella] of pulling his gun on a driver and violating the 26-year-old's civil rights.*
>
> *"….We take little pleasure in today's guilty verdict," said U.S. Attorney Damon Martinez, explaining that his office believes the vast majority of law enforcement officers are good public servants.*

Note how the prosecutor feels the need to praise other policemen when he prosecutes one of their colleagues.

Sheriff Rodella had quite a colorful work history, one that could have predicted the serious problem of aggression for which he would later be convicted. He grossly violated his law enforcement code of conduct with an incredibly wide range of misbehavior, including financial impropriety. Unfortunately, these earlier grave transgressions were either ignored or inadequately dealt with by his supervisors:

> ....*It wasn't the first time Rodella has been accused of misconduct. Two other drivers testified that they had similar encounters with Rodella, although no federal charges were filed in either case....*
>
> *Last year, the FBI searched the sheriff's office to investigate whether his staff accepted donations to a scholarship fund and then looked the other way on donors' traffic offenses.... No charges were ever filed.*
>
> *Two years before being elected sheriff in 2010, Rodella was ousted as a magistrate judge by the state Supreme Court for several alleged infractions, including promising to rule in favor of campaign supporters during a rent dispute. The court barred him from running again for judicial office.*
>
> *....During his time on the force, Rodella was disciplined for marijuana use, improper use of a weapon, falsifying official reports, abusing sick leave and using his position for personal gain, according to state reports....he was suspended for 30 days for firing at a deer decoy...set up to catch poachers.* [1]

It's hard to imagine that a teacher could survive in her profession with a rap sheet a fraction that long or serious!

Rodella, on the other hand, was able to *retire on a disability pension after 13 years*!

6. MIAMI GARDENS, FLORIDA, 2013: *THE DEVIL MAKES WORK FOR IDLE HANDS*

The owners of convenience stores often fear for their safety and that of their employees. But what is it that can cause an owner in a rough neighborhood to fear not robbers but the very police who are supposed to protect him?

Julie Brown of *The Miami Herald* reports on why a store owner installed cameras and what he found on the tapes. As with the earlier columnist, Fred Grimm, the reporter here is simply flabbergasted. Note her incredulity about the police behavior she discovered on reviewing those tapes:

> *Miami Gardens police have arrested [Earl] Sampson 62 times for one offense: trespassing. Almost every citation was issued at the same place: the 207 Quickstop, a convenience store…But Sampson isn't loitering. He works as a clerk at the Quickstop. So how can he be trespassing when he works there?*
>
> *It's a question the store's owner, Alex Saleh, 36, has been asking for more than a year as he watched Sampson, his other employees and his customers, day after day, being stopped and frisked by Miami Gardens police. Most of them, like Sampson, are poor and black.*

And like Sampson, many of them have been cited for minor infractions, sometimes as often as three times in the same day. Saleh was so troubled by what he saw that he decided to install video cameras in his store. Not to protect himself from criminals…to protect him and his customers from police.

….Those tapes…raise some troubling questions about the conduct of the city's police officers.

The videos show, among other things, cops stopping citizens, questioning them, aggressively searching them and arresting them for trespassing when they have permission to be on the premises; officers conducting searches of Saleh's business without search warrants or permission; using what appears to be excessive force on subjects who are clearly not resisting arrest and filing inaccurate police reports in connection with the arrests. [li]

Some of the cops were so brazen that they even performed some of their illegal acts specifically for the videos. Some, for example, illegally seized the beer customers had bought and emptied it on the sidewalk, grandstanding and hamming it up for the camera. This behavior certainly demonstrates impunity yet again.

The widespread tolerance for police misbehavior is what generates this impunity. Society tolerates boys behaving badly but not girls speaking up for their rights. Cops are viewed like the football players whose rowdiness and randy-ness we must amusedly tolerate for them to win the game. Teachers are viewed like the cheerleaders whose virtue must always be questioned.

7. <u>SOUTH FLORIDA, 2012</u>: *COOKING THE BOOKS*

The title of another *Miami Herald* article indicates a troubling development: "South Florida Police Officers Seem To Be Increasingly Finding Themselves on the Wrong Side of the Law." The examples cited in the article include one sheriff charged with *witness tampering*, another accused of "*shaking down* pain clinic customers and *stealing drugs and cash*," and a third arrested for driving *120 mph* on the turnpike. A fourth officer pleaded guilty to *falsifying a DUI-crash investigation* while the fifth and sixth were being investigated for "*trumping up criminal charges*" against a stranded motorist.

The seventh and eight officers were under investigation for *grand theft* while the ninth and tenth were arrested for *falsifying reports.*

What has been the response to the pattern of misbehavior noted by the reporter? Responding to all of these cases, the head of the Miami police union said, "...the public is being exposed to cases that are blown way out of proportion....just like any individual charged with a crime...a police officer is innocent until proven guilty." [lii]

President Obama, quick to criticize the good, dedicated teachers of Central Falls, Rhode Island, did not feel it was necessary to comment on this crime spree by those sworn to protect us. No politician attacked the police union for defending these criminal cops.

8. Opa-Locka, Florida, 2012: *No Wonder He Loves His Job!*

As mentioned before, one of the serious charges levelled against teachers unions is that it is supposedly very hard to fire teachers for bad performance or misconduct. Let's again take a look at this issue with respect to the police. Julie K. Brown of the *Miami Herald* reports about the following long and extraordinary career—one that apparently has no end:

> *Sgt. German Bosque....has been accused of cracking the head of a handcuffed suspect, beating juveniles, hiding drugs in his police car, stealing from suspects, defying direct orders and lying and falsifying police reports. He once called in sick to take a vacation to Cancun and has engaged in a rash of unauthorized police chases, including one in which four people were killed.*
>
> *....Now under suspension pending yet another investigation into misconduct, Bosque stays home and collects his $60,000 paycheck for doing nothing....He boldly brags about his ability to work a law enforcement system that allows bad cops to keep their certification even in the face of criminal charges.*
>
> *....his disciplinary record and his city's inability to get rid of him are a study in how legal loopholes allow troubled cops to stay on the street. Probably the most*

extraordinary aspect of Bosque's tenure with the force is that he actually managed to be promoted to sergeant... [liii]

Note, first, the language. A clearly bad cop is called "troubled." In all the criticisms of teachers, was there one who was ever called "troubled?" This discrepancy in reference is not an accident. Documented problematic cops are passed off as complexly "troubled" males, whereas merely supposedly problematic teachers are just simply "bad" women.

Next, where is the outcry against the practice of allowing suspended cops under investigation to stay home and collect their pay? Contrast this silence with the outrage— e.g., in the movie *Waiting for Superman*—about accused teachers being "coddled" for having to work in the famed "Book Depository" while under investigation.

More importantly, I have never heard of a teacher who has killed a student. And if one has indeed done so, she certainly has not been able to keep her job in the way that Bosque managed to regain his career after his speeding killed four civilians. Note that there can be no claim of self-defense here; this is not about killing suspects.

Moreover, it is certain that no teacher with a fraction of the record trailing Bosque has ever been *promoted*. With this in mind, why is there such a clamor for firing "bad" teachers and not one for firing the cops around the nation who behave like Bosque?

Finally, it is notable that it was the Miami-Dade police union that paid for the legal fights to have Bosque successfully reinstated repeatedly. No politician made a negative comment about this police union for supporting such a bad apple.

9. Broward County, Florida, 2013: *Zombies Back from the Dead!*

Sgt. Bosque above may have been an extreme case, but it is hardly unusual for bad police officers to be reinstated after being fired. Such firings, of course, only take place after officers have exhausted lengthy due process and all of their employee rights. Reinstating such fired officers is usually due to *union pressure*, as in Bosque's case above. However, there are other ways for fired police officers to regain their jobs.

In Broward County, several deputies fired for abuses to the public were rehired when one police chief was replaced by another. The chief who fired them, Sheriff Al Lamberti, complained that *"safety and life and death" issues were being ignored.* [liv] Apparently, no filmmaker thought that the lives of American civilians were important enough to make a *Waiting for Superman*-type movie about this—the national phenomenon of reinstating abusive police officers fired for good cause including danger to the public.

10. Sanford, Florida, 2011: *Official Duties: Hide and Seek, Naptime, Two Lunches, and Parties! Avoid Paperwork!*

George Zimmerman, the criminal justice major made infamous for killing Trayvon Martin in 2012, had some earlier volunteer experiences with police officers that undoubtedly help to explain why he became an over-zealous civilian vigilante. As part of his interest and training in law enforcement, Zimmerman had gone on "ride-alongs" with the Sanford police. What Zimmerman experienced severely disappointed him, resulting in a January 2011 complaint about *police laziness* to a City Hall community forum—a year *before* he killed Trayvon Martin.

Zimmermann's own words are telling:

> *...what I saw was disgusting...The officer showed me his favorite hiding spots for taking naps, explained to me that he doesn't carry a long gun in his vehicle because, in his words "anything that requires a long gun requires a lot of paperwork, and you're going to find me as far away from it."*
>
> *....He [the officer] took two lunch breaks and attended a going away party for one of his fellow officers.* [lv]

For all the dereliction of duty that teachers are accused of, there is none that matches this! Zimmermann's words were uttered a year *before* his killed Trayvon Martin, so they are not an attempt to excuse his aggression toward Trayvon.

With the wisdom of hindsight, we can see that Zimmermann's earlier frustration actually help to explain his later aggression. It is thus quite possible that an innocent teenager is dead because a citizen became overzealous due to the laziness of cops. This is probably why Zimmerman did not "stand down" when the dispatcher told him to let the police handle the questioning of Trayvon. Zimmerman may have doubted that a Sanford cop would even show up.

Notice that this connection between police laziness in Sanford and Zimmerman's hyper-reactiveness has not been drawn by the very same media that quickly attribute all sorts of negative social phenomena to teachers. Newspapers are bound to report the news—as in the instances of gross police misbehavior about which we are reading. Reporters on the ground are very diligent in ferreting out this type of corruption and misconduct. But what happens after that?

Whether newspaper editors build on their reporters' work by making the connections that are implicit in those various pieces of news depends on their editorial policy. This editorial policy emerges from the attitudes of news editors to the subjects they cover, attitudes that are formed by the society in which those editors live and also by the perspectives of the corporate owners who employ the editors.

Favorable attitudes to the police have resulted in newspapers failing to connect the dots in police misbehavior until recently. Conversely, negative attitudes to teachers have resulted in teachers being blamed for phenomena like student dropout, for which they are not responsible. Negative attitudes to teachers have similarly resulted in their workplaces being derogatorily labelled "failing schools" simply because they are located in distressed communities where student motivation is low and family and community support for education is minimal.

11. PLANTATION, FLORIDA, 2011: *SHARPENING PROMOTION SKILLS: READING, WRITING, AND A LITTLE PUBLIC OUTREACH.*

If you think that the cop above who tooled around with Zimmerman was an anomaly, consider this case of Plantation police officer Joseph Sposa. Lisa J. Huriash writes about Sposa's earnestness in carrying out his important police duties:

> *A veteran police officer [Joseph Sposa] has been suspended for 16 hours without pay for texting a domestic violence victim, asking her to lunch and to ride on his motorcycle, and telling her that her toe nail polish is "quite a turn on."….His texts show he said that <u>while on duty he mostly parks and reads</u>.*
>
> *Among other texts: "Have you ever dated an Aries?" "I have a beautiful black and chrome Harley. Black is my favorite color…Would you ride on the back?... I don't drive fast LOL."* [lvi]

As one can guess, the many such cases of police idling and shirking their duties have not prompted condemnations from the media, the public, nor the president.

12. MIAMI BEACH, 2011: *BOYS JUST WANT TO HAVE FUN!*

The July 4 weekend is usually a time when cops crack down on drunken or otherwise impaired motorists who threaten the citizenry. But what happens when it's the cops—both at the top and in the ranks—who are boozing it up on duty or disappearing from assigned stations during this busy weekend? The *Miami Herald* has the answer:

> ...*police commanders, supervisors and police officers went off the radar for hours at a time, arrived late, left early, lied about their whereabouts, <u>collected money for hours they didn't work</u> and altered time records...*
>
> *...investigation...showed a massive breakdown in command, <u>gross negligence and neglect of duty</u>—with supervisors and commanders looking the other way as officers on midnight patrol were given free rein to party in uniform and on duty...*
>
> *...the Miami Beach Police Department has been criticized for being out of control, with cops accused over the past couple of years of <u>partying on duty</u>, using excessive force, bashing gays and...wounding four bystanders...*
>
> *[Officers] Derick Kulian and Rolando Gutierrez were in uniform and on duty...when they entered the Clevelander bar about 5 a.m. They met four women celebrating a bachelorette party and began dancing with them....Kulian invited bride-to be Adalee Martin to ride on his ATV, and the two sped off down the beach with the ATV lights off. They ran over two beachgoers ... [who] suffered <u>serious injuries</u>.* [lvii]

Both officers who injured the beachgoers had been *drinking*. Witnesses said that the ATV was going at a phenomenal speed. And yet, President Obama did not comment on this Miami Beach episode nor on the Miami Beach police department. He did not even find it important to comment on the behavior of the specific officer who seriously injured the civilians on his high-speed joyride. Contrast this with his denunciation of the Central Falls teachers, none of whom were accused of negligence or shirking contracted duties.

13. PUERTO RICO, 2010: *WELL, IF YOU CAN'T BEAT THEM, JOIN THEM!*

In early October of 2010, the FBI flew hundreds of agents into Puerto Rico to arrest *eighty-nine* police officers whom they accused of various crimes involving drug trafficking. Some of the specific charges included *smuggling drugs into jail, extortion, selling bullets called "cop-killers," and even murder.*

Reacting to the arrests, one resident of Puerto Rico's capital, San Juan, said that citizens had so distrusted the police that he personally would never stop if pulled over by a cop until he got back to his own neighborhood. A San Juan attorney, Judith Berkan, commented:

> *…there has <u>never been a sense of accountability</u> in the police department….What exists in pure impunity, so much so that it is very common for police officers in Puerto Rico to openly violate the law… I have seen corrupt police officers, violent officers, <u>gangs operating in the police</u>….With these arrests, they are just scratching the surface.* [lviii]

Reflect on that. The arrest of *eighty-nine* police officers is merely just scratching the surface of a problem in one police force!

The secretary of the Puerto Rico police union, while admitting that there was no justification for breaking the law, explained the corruption by saying that officers were *paid too little*. US Attorney General Eric Holder insisted after the arrests that the majority of Puerto Rico's Police were honest and reassured police officers that "We will not allow the corrupt actions of a few to undermine *the good work* of so many or to derail the great progress that you've worked to achieve." President Obama again did not comment on the police abuse. Silence can indeed be deafening!

14. CAMDEN, NEW JERSEY, 2010: *THE GANGS WERE BETTER!*

In April 2010, prosecutors in Camden had to drop charges or vacate convictions in 185 cases because of widespread police misconduct. Residents had complained for years that police had bullied them, "planted drugs on suspects," stole cash, falsified police reports, and conducted illegal searches. In March, one officer admitted such crimes in court.

However, residents maintained that the problem was much more widespread, with officers greeting residents by punching them and routinely framing innocents on drug crimes, for which some spent extensive time in jail. In the words of a Camden resident, *"The cops were more of a problem than the crime was!"* [lix]

Camden has one of the highest crime rates in the United States. The police abuse came to light in a situation that developed after 2008 when police *"started using more sophisticated data to figure out when and where crime was the highest….to make sure they had more officers on the streets at those times."*

Commenting on the revelations, the Camden Police Chief maintained that the abuses were committed by, "a *very small* group of criminals with badges." The president of the Camden police union similarly asserted that, "Just because one person pled guilty, it doesn't mean that everybody is guilty." Neither US Attorney General Holder nor President Obama saw fit to comment on this police abuse.

15. HOLLYWOOD, FLORIDA, VARIOUS YEARS: *WELL, AT LEAST THEY WERE GUARDING SOMETHING!*

I teach in Hollywood, Florida, which bills itself as the "small town on the beach." Beneath this idyllic facade, however, are continual revelations of wrongdoing by some members of the Hollywood police force.

In February 2007, for example, four Hollywood policemen were charged with *delivering heroin* in a FBI sting. These four, who were later convicted, were part of a larger group whose other members survived the sting because top Hollywood cops, when alerted to the investigation by the FBI, *warned their errant colleagues*!

The corrupt cops who were caught even *guarded drug shipments*, with their police cruisers blaring their sirens to ensure undisturbed passage of drugs and supposed mob couriers. One investigating FBI agent commented, "What was amazing to me is that it was *so easy to get cops to look the other way*, to guard trucks for us, no questions asked. I'd never seen anything like it." [lx]

A few years ago, four Hollywood policemen falsified a crash report in which one of them rear-ended a female driver. The intent was to cast the blame on the woman by falsely claiming that a cat had leapt out of her vehicle causing the accident. The cover-up came to light in a review of the patrol car's tape which had recorded one officer discussing with the others how to "do a little Walt Disney to protect the cop." [lxi]

One official of the police union reacted by asserting that, "When the facts come to light, I'm sure all of... [the accused officers] will be exonerated." The police union issued a statement calling the intended firing of the officers, "a public lynching." Neither US Attorney General Holder nor President Barack Obama has commented about *continuous revelations of police corruption* in Hollywood, Florida.

16. MIAMI, FLORIDA, 1979: *SORRY! NO HUMOR HERE!*

Let us now go back further in time to see that the behavior described above is really not just a recent phenomenon but rather part of a long-standing pattern. We will also see that such gross misbehavior has been evident and tolerated for a long time.

On December 17, 1979, an unemployed insurance agent named Arthur McDuffie led Miami police on an 8-minute, high-speed chase through city streets while riding a motorcycle. He ended up being beaten to death. The coroner reported he had never seen such brain damage in thousands of cases.

The five police officers who had arrested McDuffie were put on trial with some turning state witnesses. They described how McDuffie was beaten and how they tried to cover it up by running over his motorcycle with the patrol car to make it look like his injuries were caused by a collision. The officers were acquitted in both state and federal trials. They were even reinstated to their jobs after the Miami Fraternal Order of Police *threatened a walkout*. [lxii]

17. Dade County, Florida, 1966: *New Sport for Police Athletic League: Fencing*

Here is an even earlier example that details *a police racket that had civilians in terror*. It confirms that there has been a *long-standing* pattern of police misbehavior that existed even before society changed during the late 1960s:

> *In 1966, the Dade County Grand Jury described a burglary racket overseen by the sheriff's office that directed criminals to residences where the booty would be lucrative and where cops, guaranteed, would be elsewhere.*
>
> *The burglars gave up a share of their loot to their cops bosses. And [Sheriff] Buchanan's boys also oversaw the fencing operations.* [lxiii]

Criminals who broke the pact were *ambushed by the cops.* The indictment described witnesses who were *"terrified for their own safety and the safety of their families."*

The only way to describe such a situation is that of a ***police state***. Its origins obviously run long and deep.

18. Miami, Florida, 2015: *Shouldn't Education Be Similarly Analyzed?*

For the final example, let us return to the present to view not another case of misconduct but how officials and experts accurately explain the real problems police face that make their work difficult. In Miami, the police success rate has *nosedived.*

Despite the numerous types of outrageous police behavior described earlier, *no one has pointed to such abuses to explain the lack of police success.* Instead, officials and experts *seriously* analyze the problems police face. The *Miami Herald* reports their balanced comments:

> *In almost four years, 646 people have been shot in Miami's inner-city. Only 94 of those cases have been cleared....the clearance rate—arrests made in shootings—has <u>declined dramatically</u>.*
>
> *Police and crime experts give myriad reasons...people won't speak. Gang fights...limit witnesses. An overtaxed police force is focused on preventing crime, resulting in fewer crimes solved....[Other causes are] past philosophies...the politics of policing...reassignments...* [lxiv]

Note *the glaring lack of witch-hunting*—not one accusatory finger pointing to police misconduct to explain the decline in performance!

It's Official: Boys Will Be Boys!

Examples #1 to #17 in the previous section are only a *small fraction* of the verified longstanding wrongdoing and failures by some police officers across the nation. Summarizing the reaction of top government officials and police chiefs to such infractions and failures is quite revealing:

1. When some policemen are caught in serious wrongdoing, police chiefs and top US law enforcement officials are quick to defend the general reputation of policemen of the particular force that was investigated.

2. Even when corruption and other wrongdoing is widespread in a particular force, police chiefs and US officials insist that only a minority of police officers are guilty.

3. Police unions automatically defend members accused of wrongdoing, even when evidence of such wrongdoing (e.g. surreptitiously videotaped incidents and confessions by the cops themselves) is indisputable.

4. Police unions successfully get verified violent police offenders reinstated after the latter have

exhausted all of their due process and employee rights. They do this by threatening illegal strikes.

5. Many bad cops who engage in repeated misconduct are even promoted.

6. Police chiefs, US law enforcement officials, and the US president do not criticize police unions for protecting specific bad cops.

7. Police chiefs, US law enforcement officials, and the US president do not condemn police unions for hindering the general cleanup of a police force.

8. Police chiefs, US law enforcement officials, and the US president do not place the blame of a city's crime rate on a police union that protected bad cops.

9. Instead of unfairly assigning blame, officials point to the real reasons, i.e., problems in society such as drugs, guns, and gangs, to explain why police do not meet crime reduction goals.

10. Similarly, when police fail to solve crimes, officials take a serious look at the fundamental causes: an "overtaxed" force, reassignments, lack of cooperation from witnesses, etc.

11. No one uses the numerous examples of police misbehavior to explain the lack of police success. No one has suggested that such chronic misbehavior and lack of success are reasons to privatize the police forces. No one suggests introducing competition to improve police productivity and performance.

12. Some officials go to extraordinary lengths to excuse police failures, such as blaming the right of citizens to record in a public area for the refusal of cops to get out of their cars and properly police neighborhoods.

What would be the reaction of government officials and neoliberal politicians if the shirkers, thieves, and bullies described above were teachers? We can well imagine. Let us therefore more explicitly compare the treatment of cops and teachers in the next section.

Condoning Cops vs. Condemning Teachers

The purpose of the recitation and discussion about policemen in the previous sections is not to condemn all cops or even a majority of them. The average policeman is indeed a decent, hardworking, committed, and competent professional. However, so is the average teacher! One reason for pointing to all the bad cops and the decline in police success is simply to *contrast the consideration with which cops are treated with the contemptuous, dismissive taunts to which teachers are subjected.* Let us now analyze these contrasts.

1. Sexism and Selective Understanding

It does indeed make perfect sense not to condemn an entire police force even when wrongdoing is widespread. Moreover, it is perfectly understandable that police unions insist on due process for their members who are accused of wrongdoing. Likewise, it is good for employee morale to show appreciation for the good work of the majority in a profession when a small minority are caught behaving delinquently. *However, why is such consideration not accorded to teachers and their unions?*

Why do officials and experts point to deeper social issues to explain the decline in police success but fail to do so for teachers in the *same failing neighborhoods*? How is it that the head of the FBI can accept cops shuttering themselves in their cars, refusing to properly police tough neighborhoods because of the fear of being videotaped while the governor of Ohio calls for teacher lounges to be abolished and a New York principal unceremoniously dumps teachers' desks and filing cabinets into the trash? The answer is quite clear—*sexism.*

We all know of areas in our cities where crime is very high. Residents of these neighborhoods live in fear while residents of other areas avoid such notorious communities. How are police precincts in such dangerous districts treated by the media? Are they considered "*failing* police precincts?" Are the cops in those precincts labeled as "*less effective* cops?" Does the President call for the *dismissal* of all employees of a precinct where the crime rate remains stubbornly high?

2. Selective Hysteria: Evaluating Cops vs. Teachers

Of course, no one ever proposes evaluating cops on the basis of the problems in the bad neighborhoods to which they are assigned. Even considering the idea would obviously be unfair and inimical to morale. Applying this logical principle to education, why are schools in the *very same* distressed neighborhoods considered "failing schools?" Why are teachers at such schools labeled "less effective" and subject to dismissal as in the case with the Central Falls teachers and counselors?

Moreover, with the multitude of accusations made against teachers, no one has ever had cause to accuse a school of routinely *promoting* ignorance or misinformation. Teachers have been accused of not doing their duty but no one has been able to accuse them of deliberately working to make their students more ignorant. *Contrast this with the charge made by some residents of New Jersey, Puerto Rico, and Florida that their cops were worse than the crime itself!*

Contrast the accusations against teachers with the FBI documenting that cops in Hollywood, Florida actually helped to deliver drugs! Contrast the non-reaction of media pundits and neoliberal politicians to such police corruption with their worked-up outrage to alleged teacher deficiencies. Why the hysteria about supposed teacher failures and silence until 2015 about documented police abuses—and then only concern about unwarranted shootings, *ignoring the myriad other abuses* such as shirking work and financial impropriety?

3. Sexism and Impossible Expectations
Apart from handling the deficiencies of cops and teachers differently, the media and government officials also have

much lower expectations for police officers than they do for educators. The following is just a minor but illustrative comparison.

Cops are *not* expected to work miracles rounding up all the criminals in bad neighborhoods, but teachers and counselors are now required to *work statistical miracles with the kids of these very same criminals.* Yes, it is a sad reality that especially in failing neighborhoods, some of the kids in school have parents, usually fathers, who are criminals.

While it is very possible for the child of a criminal not to be fated to follow in the path of his parent, the interventions by social workers that make such turnarounds possible have been sabotaged by neoliberal budget cuts. As a consequence, some of the "kids" of criminals—though in school—are unfortunately often well on the road to similar familial delinquency by the time they reach high school. Without intensive support from the social services, schools and teachers simply cannot counteract the malignant influence of some families and certain peer groups in the communities, no matter how hard they may try.

Totally ignoring the social dysfunction in some communities, the requirements of *No Child Left Behind* and its successors such as *Race To The Top* insist that *every* child must achieve competence in English and Math—*whether or not he or she wants to!* The new *Common Core* curriculum and tests demand success in a multitude of subjects. Even though the kids of criminals are a small minority in a distressed neighborhood, they make the goals of these absolutist laws *statistically impossible to achieve.* Moreover, the behavior of these juvenile criminals in schools makes teaching difficult for teachers and also renders learning difficult for those students who do want to learn.

When these juvenile criminals drop out of school to pursue their more remunerative illegal activities full-time, it is the schools that get the blame for the dropout rate and for "failing" to keep them in school. But what about the parents who tolerate the illegal behavior that leads to the dropout? What about the peer groups in the community that encourage such criminality and the dropping out? Most importantly, what about the fundamental cause: the injustice of the larger society that creates the dysfunctions of such failing communities and the individuals in them?

While most students who drop out are not criminals, they also have been too beaten down in their failing communities and dysfunctional families to see any hope in education. After all, they hardly see adults around them in their community gainfully employed. Societal reasons for student failure are thus ignored.

Teachers and schools are instead blamed for the poor academic performance or dropping out of juveniles but the cops are not blamed when they fail to prevent these juveniles from committing crimes. Schools are somehow expected to miraculously keep students in school as if it were a jail, but cops are not expected to, say, stop motorists from committing traffic offences. The double standard for the female profession as compared to the male one is glaring!

Here is yet another issue worthy of comparison. Isn't a person's physical safety—his very life—even more important that his education? So why isn't there a law mandating requirements for public safety—a *No Criminal Left Behind* law that mandates that by the target date of 2020, *every criminal will be behind bars and every community will be crime-free?*

The opinions of conservatives such as Pat Buchanan and Georg Will, who are no friends of teachers or their unions, are refreshingly frank and insightful on mandated education requirements. They have declared the *No Child Left Behind* mandate of universal student competence in English and Math as absurdly utopian—just as absurd as the equivalent requirement of a national crime-free environment would be. And yet, while the latter is sensibly never considered, the former exists and is punitively enforced. Why?

4. GENDER: SUPPORT VS. BLAME

Since discrepancies in the treatment of cops and teachers lie in gender and role differences, let us dissect this issue of roles more closely. Policing requires attributes and behavior traditionally associated with masculinity: physical prowess, combativeness, and use of weapons. Teaching, on the other hand, is associated with traditionally feminine qualities and actions: empathy, caring, and working with kids. As the English folk saying at the beginning of this chapter indicates, *unrealistic demands are not made of men whereas impossible demands are routinely and unthinkingly demanded of women.*

Even though some teachers are male, the fact that they have chosen a nurturing, traditionally female profession means that they will be treated with the same disrespect that befalls women. Conversely, female police officers are deemed by society to have earned the respect due to males by dint of the macho training they have endured and the physical dangers they face in their line of work.

The unrealistic demands made of women derive from the historical devaluing of the difficulty of women's work. *This devaluing, coupled with the tendency to blame women for problems (as in Salem), explains why teachers are despised and maligned today for the state of American education.* The teachers who have the most difficult students in the most difficult areas get blamed for the very conditions of their work, for the very difficulty of their tasks!

Teachers' complaints about the impossibility of the expectations placed on them are not taken seriously for the same reason that doctors do not take the complaints of female patients as seriously as those of men. (A study done a few years back showed that when women complained about pain to doctors, they were taken less seriously than when men did so.)

The converse historical respect for men's work is reflected in how society treats cops in tough neighborhoods. They have the sympathy of the media and the public as well as the support of those in power. Review the article about the Camden cops quoted earlier. Note that to deal with the extensive crime that traditionally exists in Camden, officials added *"more officers on the streets"* during peak crime hours. *When faced with a difficult problem, the cops were supported, not condemned.*

More teachers were *not* sent to Rigoberto's Elementary School in East Los Angeles. More teachers were *not* sent to Central Falls High School in Rhode Island. Rigoberto was instead condemned by an online metric and the Central Falls teachers were condemned by the President himself for not wanting to put in extra hours without due compensation. The attitude of the media and politicians was that rather than expect help, they should have just worked a little harder. As the old ditty introducing this chapter goes, "A man works from sun-up to sundown, but a woman's work is never done."

5. SEXISM AND OVERTIME

The differing expectations for cops versus teachers recall the sexist dichotomy that society presents to a woman: *if you reject being the virtuous, self-sacrificing angel, you will be labeled a malevolent witch.* Another glaring example of this sexist difference in expectations for the two professions lies in the attitude of supervisory officials and politicians toward overtime pay.

Politicians and the respective supervisors of the police and teaching professions expect the following: *cops will claim the famed overtime pay that really ratchets up their pensions while teachers will sacrifice their free time without compensation.* Thus, if a rash of burglaries or a mini-riot breaks out in a violent precinct, the cops who have to extend their shift will, without any controversy at all, be able to claim overtime pay. No one expects these cops to work the required extra hours for free. No one says, "You must contribute your time to solve this problem now because it was your earlier lack of diligent policing that resulted in this current crisis of criminality!"

Contrast this with the extra duties expected of teachers and performed by teachers without extra pay and, more importantly, *without complaint*: grading papers at home, coaching clubs and sports, escorting students on after-hours field trips or excursions, attending meetings and parent conferences after school, attending workshops and pursuing professional growth, and so on *ad infinitum*.

However, teachers do defy the sexist expectation of submissive acceptance of extra duties when superintendents and school boards arbitrarily assign extra teaching and supervisory duties without adequate compensation. This is what was at the heart of the problem in Central Falls, Rhode Island. The superintendent and school board responsible for Central Falls determined that (1) students there needed a longer school day; (2) students needed the guidance of teachers during lunch; and (3) teachers needed extra training during the summer. *The teachers union agreed to all of this* but asked—like any police union would—that there be extra pay for mandated extra work. This was a big mistake, coming as it was from a traditionally female profession.

The media's treatment of the union's request for fair compensation reveals indeed the continuing devaluation of women's work. The proposed supervision of students during lunch was portrayed as a pleasant, almost bucolic family experience. The reality, however, is that during lunch, especially in tough areas like Central Falls, the cafeteria resembles the demilitarized zone between North and South Korea. On second thought, it doesn't. Though tense, that demilitarized zone is extremely quiet. A school cafeteria in a failing neighborhood at lunch rather resembles Baghdad at the height of the Iraqi insurgency.

Adults in the cafeteria have to ensure that the floors are not mopped with milk—the mops being students' shoes deliberately kicking milk cartons—and that the walls are not smeared with food. They have to ensure the proper return or disposal of trays, utensils, and food. In particular, they have to make sure that students don't dispose of utensils by sticking them into each other!

Staff stationed in the cafeteria—"stationed" in the military sense is the correct word—have to prevent food fights, which turn into mini-riots, from breaking out. I well recall students in my class receiving mass text messages about an activity scheduled to start in fifteen minutes, the beginning of the lunch period. Those messages promised—and urged participation in—food fights involving different campus groups. Adults in the cafeteria also have to prevent (1) real fights between gangs or gang wannabees, (2) histrionic, emotional screaming contests between former lovers, and (3) physical fights between jilted revenge seekers and the new lovers of their ex-partners.

The school cafeteria is where all students meet. In a tough neighborhood, a high school cafeteria is where that small minority who have already committed *violent crimes* and exhibited *mental illness* also meet, *unrestrained by the institutions* that will later separate them from those of you who are not teachers.

Unless you are a cop, a jailer, or a psychiatric nurse, you really do not know what teachers have to put up with in both the cafeteria and the classroom—all without the benefit of the resources and sanctions that cops, jailers, and psychiatric nurses can call on. It was therefore far from unreasonable for the Central Falls teachers union to ask for compensation for teachers mandated to eat lunch in the cafeteria. The following news articles— from opposite ends of the country—illustrate the reality of lunch at an inner-city school cafeteria. First, the West Coast:

> *Three Sacramento-area high school students were arrested after a principal was <u>slammed to the floor</u> during a melee that was recorded on video…The video shows students yelling and running while others frantically climb onto tables….a student wrestled with Principal Don Ross and violently shoved him to the floor….*
>
> *Three school officials were injured and needed medical attention….10-12 students were involved in two separate incidents…In the first incident, eight to 10 students were fighting over a week-old dispute about a relationship….Later, another brawl broke out between two students…* [lxv]

Now, the East Coast:

> *A fight...in the Miami Springs High cafeteria ended with one of the students going on a rampage....the student <u>swung at everyone</u>, including a cafeteria worker and a police officer. Students jumped on cafeteria tables...*
>
> *...when a cafeteria worker, vice principal and security guard tried to intervene, they became victims themselves....[A student said] "One of the policemen came in and the kid punched him."...The student who was arrested is charged with battery on a law enforcement officer.* [lxvi]

On second thought, the Central Falls teachers should really not have asked for regular pay for cafeteria duty; they should have demanded **combat pay!**

The media's treatment of the longer workday required of Central Falls teachers was as dismissive as its treatment of cafeteria duty. Commentators often pointed out that only twenty-five minutes had been added to the teacher workday. It was not mentioned that with those extra twenty-five minutes, there would be extra homework to be graded at home—especially given the more exacting curriculum and test preparation that would be implemented.

Similarly, the media and government officials were hostile to the Central Falls teachers' request to be compensated for summer training. They ignored the fact that many teachers often work summer jobs to supplement their pay. Even critics of teachers acknowledge that teacher pay does not come close to the pay of other professionals with similar education.

Was it thus fair to expect the Central Falls teachers to forego this summer income for unpaid specialized teacher training that was necessary due to the difficulty of their jobs? After all, the cops in Central Falls are paid to attend the special trainings they need in order to deal with the drug infestation in that very same city. Likewise, when these officers have to extend their shifts *to arrest some parents of Central Falls students*, they are paid overtime without any question asked at all by supervisors and nary a comment made by the media or neoliberal politicians.

In the Central Falls negotiations between the school board and the teachers union, the focus on additional teacher pay revealed that *teacher competence was really not the issue at all*. After they were all fired, all of the educators at Central Falls were eventually rehired—*once they agreed to do the extra work without extra pay*!

The rehiring of all teachers gave the lie to Obama's and Duncan's comments that teacher incompetence was responsible for the firings. Rather, the teachers and counselors were fired because *they rejected the role of the self-sacrificing angelic females.* They had the temerity to insist instead on compensation for mandated extra hours—at a regular rate *lower* than the overtime rate which cops routinely receive without question.

Some media commentators claimed, however, that teachers should not expect extra pay for the newly mandated extra work because their salaries were so much higher than that of the average resident of poverty-stricken Central Falls! Has there ever been a similar comment made about cops—that overtime pay should be denied because they make so much more than the denizens of the alleyways they police?

6. Sexism and Accepting the Abuse of Teachers

Note that the violently enraged student in the Florida cafeteria described above was *only charged with battery on the police officer,* ignoring his attacks on school personnel. Apparently, school employees have to accept being beaten up by students. Once again, women have to tolerate abuse. Indeed, daily student abuse of teachers is a serious problem that causes many teachers to leave the profession.

Conclusion: The Old Double-Standard

As we have seen, there is great disparity in the treatment of teachers versus police officers regarding pay, performance expectations, the deficiencies of a minority in each profession, and the toleration of abuse. This disparity exists because of the double standard—*the sexist expectation that teachers should not be accorded the same rights and respect as public safety professionals* such as cops or firefighters. Instead, teachers—having chosen a "feminine" profession—are expected to be totally self-sacrificing angels. This is the Florence Nightingale-like sacrifice demanded of women.

Teachers who are faced with the difficulty of teaching students in a failing neighborhood are expected to sacrifice like the heroic teacher in *Stand and Deliver*. This teacher prototype, repeated in many inspirational teaching films, is the educational equivalent of Florence Nightingale in totally sacrificing his time, relationships, and marriage to his profession. This was the standard demanded of the entire staff of Central Falls by President Obama, Secretary of Education Duncan, and the superintendent and board of education for Central Falls.

Apart from the sexist inequity of such an expectation, there is also the problem that even when such sacrifice is made, it is not appreciated because of the unrealistic expectations that the mostly male education officials have of teachers. Rigoberto Ruelas Jr. was a real life educational equivalent of Florence Nightingale. He dedicated all his time and effort to his school. When even this could not counteract the deleterious educational effects of the decaying community in which he taught, he was nevertheless humiliated for being "less effective."

The external causes of Rigoberto's death were public humiliation, the denunciation of teachers in the media, and the sanctioning of collective punishment by both his ultimate boss, Arne Duncan, and his president, Barack Hussein Obama. The internal causes of Rigoberto's death were his own super-dedication and over-sacrifice—the very same qualities still being demanded of those teachers who have not yet, in despair, followed him into the forgiving void of oblivion.

CHAPTER 12

—— ✏ ——

Why Teachers and Not Bankers?
The Panama Papers Hypocrisy

There are those who protect society's injustice with a gun,
And there are those who protect it with a pen.
The latter are more deadly.

IN APRIL 2016, journalists in the International Consortium of Investigative Journalists revealed how corporations and the wealthy avoid taxes by banking in offshore tax havens like Panama. They implicated politicians around the world, forcing the Prime Minister of Iceland to resign.

What the parent newspapers did not do was to detail the severe effects of such tax avoidance. By banking offshore, the super-rich deprive their countries of much needed funds to help society function properly. Much of the decay of society—including its schools—is indeed the result of various legal and illegal stratagems used by the rich to avoid taxes.

As Elizabeth Warren and Robert Reich have pointed out, the wealthy make their millions by using the roads society has constructed in order to ship their goods. They use the schools that society maintains to educate their workforce. However, when it comes time to contribute to the upkeep of the very roads and schools that make them wealthy, the rich manifest a sudden desire to be independent of their society.

Our corporate media facilitates such illegal and selfish irresponsibility. Though releasing the names of public figures, the investigating newspapers nevertheless refused to divulge the names of private wealthy individuals who engage in offshore tax evasion. Such disclosure was considered an invasion of privacy and not deemed to be in the public interest.

Once again, the corporate media protects the wealthy at the expense of society and the poor. Contributing to the revenue starvation of society and the government is apparently not an issue of the public interest. Disclosing who is responsible for decaying infrastructure and schools is evidently not in the public interest.

However, our corporate media considers it very much in the public interest to disclose the name of a modest-income teacher like Rigoberto Ruelas Jr.

Rigoberto's impoverished students lived in a neighborhood that is failing because it is starved of taxes due to neoliberal austerity. Rigoberto's old school is "failing" because it is similarly deprived of the taxes that offshore banking circumvents. Neoliberal politicians implement the crippling budget cuts and permit such offshore tax avoidance in order to pay back those who finance their campaigns. In doing so, they made Rigoberto's job impossible.

Despite his intense and time-consuming dedication, Rigoberto couldn't overcome the effects of the urban poverty created by neoliberal politicians, bankers, and wealthy tax-dodgers. He couldn't get his deprived, alienated students to pass their state-imposed exams. *The same media which protects its rich corporate owners who bank offshore nevertheless publicly broadcast this poor public teacher's name as an* **ineffective teacher** *for all to see.*

There are those who protect society's injustice with a gun and those who protect it with a pen. In suppressing the parts of the *Panama Papers* that implicate wealthy individual tax-dodgers, our corporate media falls among the latter. Once again, the rich get away with their selfish, anti-social behavior that severely sabotages communities and schools while the poor and the weak are scapegoated for the effects of this sabotage of the rich.

As in Salem, our accused witches of today—teachers— pay the price for the elite who bleed their patients dry.

CHAPTER 13

— ❧ —

Three Witch-Hunting Myths

IN ANY SERIOUS professional field, before any proposed changes are made, all evidence is considered and policy issues are thoroughly reasoned out without the use of sloganeering. This is because such changes will affect the field, the clients, the professionals, and the public—often in serious ways. *This careful, scientific, professional process is totally jettisoned in education.*

Because most education workers are women and because the clients are kids, neoliberal education "reformers" are able to push through rash changes by (1) manipulating the general public which is understandably concerned about their kids and (2) playing on sexist disregard for the rights of women. By claiming that the witches are harming the kids, "reformers" are able to forcibly implement destructive changes. Their trumpeting of such harm lets them get away with unchallenged shallow criticisms and supposedly self-evident truths that are actually demonstrably false.

This chapter therefore answers charges leveled against American teachers and public education. The "reform" criticisms and myths are developed as critical questions in *italics*. The answers I have provided show that many denunciations of teachers and public education which may seem valid at first glance actually *ignore important, undisputed evidence* that would negate the criticisms. In ramming through education "reform," this evidence is ignored—to the detriment of public education—in order to further increase the bottom lines of those who benefit from privatizing our school system.

Myth #1:
Waiting for Superman Proves Teachers Ruin Education

> *Didn't the movie <u>Waiting for Superman</u> show that good students who are poor but want to learn are hurt by bad teachers who just don't care?*

The basic problem with *Waiting for Superman (WFS)* is its selectivity in the choice of material it presents. It is not an impartial documentary but rather a highly tailored advocacy piece that seeks to promote a certain viewpoint by tearing at our emotions.

There is nothing wrong with advocacy in general. *The Teacher's Manifesto*, after all, advocates for the rights of those subjected to injustice. As the writer of this book, however, I have made it clear that the book comes from the perspective of a teacher. *WFS*, on the other hand, *pretends* to be an objective look at education. In this, it is misleading.

WFS is actually dangerously misleading because while pretending to be objective, it does what propagandists do best: *manipulate the emotions*. The film's manipulation of our emotions is particularly effective because *it exploits the basic human concern for kids*. This manipulation is especially masterful in its depiction of the hopes, fears, and disappointments of children who are vulnerable.

1. WITCH-HUNTING ON TAPE

In *WFS*, we see good students and bad teachers. The good students were selected because they are good; the bad teachers were selected because they are bad. The good students know they are being filmed; the bad teachers do not. What sort of balanced impression about education does one expect to get from that?

For a truer look at what happens in the classroom, students and teachers need to be filmed without either knowing that this is occurring. A representative selection of the raw tapes should then be used to make the documentary. This would more approximate an impartial scientific study. We know what we would find were this to happen in an inner-city public school. So does the producer of *WFS*.

What we would find in a representative documentary about education are some of the school "incidents" that make the news—including the police reports—of the daily newspapers. (See the last section of Chapter Eleven for reports of such "incidents" in public school cafeterias across the nation.)

What we would find in a balanced film are some students—the type conveniently ignored by *WFS*—who are the total opposite of the dedicated students portrayed. We would find the former making the lives of the latter unbearable. We would find them sabotaging the education of the dedicated students with intimidation and disruption. The film producer consequently rejects a broad, neutral approach of covering the fundamental problems in education because it would contradict the specific point he intends to make.

Instead of using a lens open to whatever it comes across, the filmmaker opts for ***a lens focused on an agenda***. *He shows the best of students and the worst of teachers—with no instructional relationship between the two groups!* The bad teachers are not even the teachers of the good students around whom the film is centered. Therefore these students' discontent with public education could not have been caused by the uncaring teachers who are portrayed.

Without providing any evidence at all, the filmmaker insinuates that the problems of the good students with whom we come to sympathize derive from the behavior of bad teachers such as the random ones we see. Again without providing any evidence, he gives the impression that the students are discontented and want to attend charter schools because of such teachers. Basically, instances of bad teaching are *pulled in from elsewhere* specifically to make the teachers of the featured students look bad. Guilt by association! The film is thus a masterpiece of *the emotional and intellectual manipulation* that good propaganda perfects.

The filmmaker synthesizes selective, unconnected, and unbalanced material to claim that the reality he presents is reflective of typical public schools and is thus a balanced look at American education that explains how teachers cause problems for their students. Again, such selectivity raises the question as to how representative his portrayal is.

Without any doubt, the filmmaker *left on his cutting board* those parts of the interviews with his featured students in which the latter complained about how rough and disruptive fellow students made them feel unsafe and hampered their education. This just did not fit in with the agenda of his film.

2. A SALEM FILM?

Imagine that the following film was made during the Salem witch hysteria. A filmmaker records the various afflictions the Salem children are exhibiting. The filmmaker then searches for some obscure, marginalized women who happen to practice a nature worship resembling witchcraft. The filmmaker then juxtaposes the two types of scenes and proclaims:

> *Ha! See? Here is the proof! The children of Salem are obviously suffering. And look! Here are women practicing witchcraft in the woods! The children must be the victims of the women of Salem, most of whom practice this sort of witchcraft!*

Film did not exist in the time of Salem, but there were witch-hunting preachers who said as much. And this is precisely the type of argument that *WFS* makes. Such is the manipulative, misleading film made by the producer of *Waiting for Superman.*

Let us look at just one of the misleading aspects of *WFS*' indictment of teachers that can easily be explained. There is a scene in which a teacher is evidently not teaching while students mingle, talk, etc. The context for this scene is not given and it is implied that this is a regular class. It could be but it is likely that it is not.

Scenes of unproductive classrooms develop because of *the massive disruption to school schedules* caused by "education reform" testing. Because of such testing disruptions, teachers or substitutes are often rescheduled to basically babysit students who are not in their classes. The teachers' own students are taking one of the myriad tests forced on them and the strange students assigned to her or to the substitute have had their own teachers reassigned to proctoring the tests.

Again, the filmmaking approach of the man who created *WFS* is nothing less than extremely skillful propaganda. Propaganda needs to be recognized as such and balanced by propaganda on the other side. Unfortunately, there are no special interests to fund the other side.

Neoliberal investors promoted the highly-biased *WFS* to make the case for charter schools that would increase their bottom line. The filmmaker created a prosecutorial indictment of teachers. No one has yet funded a film defending teachers. *The Teacher's Manifesto* is an attempt to counteract the harmful witch-hunting slant of *Waiting for Superman*—the type of dangerous slant that resulted in the death of Rigoberto Ruelas Jr.

WFS is eerily reminiscent of the medieval indictment of women called *Witches' Hammer* which similarly resulted in the deaths of innocents. In its manipulation of the emotions of those concerned about children, *WFS* also reincarnates the demagogic tradition of the Salem witch hunters who similarly claimed to be protecting children.

Waiting for Superman is powerful and compelling. It is also blatantly one-sided and grossly misleading. It is therefore very effectively *a revival of the vicious witch-hunting tracts of old* that blame women for hurting kids.

3. A WORK OF GUILT

Who produced such a film as *Waiting for Superman*? Why?

WFS was made by Davis Guggenheim of the fabulously wealthy Guggenheim family, the same one that created the vast philanthropical foundation of that name. Davis Guggenheim himself is worth *2.5 billion dollars!*

WFS is without doubt a product of **liberal guilt:** Guggenheim says that he was motivated to make the film because *he felt guilty driving his kids to a private school* while seeing poor kids going to a much inferior public school in a troubled neighborhood.

Instead of addressing this underlying problem of poverty and the dysfunctions it creates in poor neighborhoods and their schools, Guggenheim takes the easy route. He attacks those who work with the poor kids he sees in the failing neighborhoods. He blames the poverty in those neighborhoods on poor schools rather than on the unjust economic system that so greatly enriches him while paying bare subsistence wages to the parents of the kids he cares about. Yes, Guggenheim actually believes that *teachers are responsible for poverty in America!* Like the Salem witches, teachers are insidiously destroying our society.

The poverty that Guggenheim cares about exists in the neighborhoods he drives by but never personally experiences. He consequently has *the sheltered liberal's idealized, naive image of the noble poor.* This idealization of the underdog lacks a mature understanding of how poverty creates dysfunctions in individuals and communities.

Guggenheim's privileged insulation explains why his film only shows the good students at the schools in failing neighborhoods. *Waiting for Superman* doesn't feature those kids who are psychically wounded by the economic system that enriches Guggenheim and who react dysfunctionally. *WFS* doesn't depict the greatest victims of Guggenheim and his social class: the disturbed students who sabotage their own education and that of their fellow students with criminal mischief and anti-social behavior.

Guggenheim created *Waiting for Superman* in an attempt to absolve himself of his admitted guilt about the privileges he and his own children enjoy at the expense of inner-city students. However, in doing so, he commits another sin by condemning an entire class of people—teachers—for the crimes of capitalism against these students. The repeated cycle of poverty versus privilege bothers Guggenheim's conscience, but *he fears to get to the bottom of it* by examining the privileges *he* inherits and passes on.

4. SELF-INTERESTED BLAME SHIFTING

Though professing concern for the poor and their education, Guggenheim's *WFS* does not suggest restoring tax rates on the rich to the levels they were under Eisenhower so that the federal government could better support local school districts. The website for the film does mention overworked teachers who are so harried that they can't adequately help students. However *WFS* fails to explore this issue and its cause: the tax cuts that have reduced funds for education, thereby forcing teachers to take on more and larger classes.

Guggenheim does not discuss restoring such taxes and funding for education. *Nothing that threatens the enlargement of Guggenheim's $2.5 billion net worth is to be considered.* Indeed, some have wondered how much of Guggenheim's $2.5 billion was earned from being strategically invested in charter schools in anticipation of the release of the film that promoted them as the solution to the problems of public schools.

For Guggenheim, it is much easier, less threatening, and certainly more rewarding to scapegoat the vulnerable than to point to an unjust economic system that creates failing communities and the neighborhood schools that naturally reflect such communities. Guggenheim thus fails the test of conscience by refusing to challenge his privileges and those of his social class.

5. Where is Superman's X-Ray Vision?

In the DC comics, Superman possesses the ability to see things that other mortals can't. His X-Ray powers of vision are deeper. Penetrating the surface distractions, Superman sees the more threatening dangers lurking beneath. Unfortunately, Guggenheim doesn't give his *Waiting for Superman* film the same degree of insight.

Instead of conducting a witch-hunt against vulnerable teachers, Guggenheim could examine the abuses of off-shore banking that enable the wealthy to avoid the taxes that public schools desperately need. Long before the release of the *Panama Papers*, Bernie Sanders thundered about this secretive privilege. Investigating offshore tax-dodging, however, would undoubtedly threaten many of Guggenheim's rich friends.

There are many other deeper issues that Guggenheim could explore. Addressing these fundamental evils would improve the communities in which *WFS's* students live and the living conditions of the families there, thereby creating better schools with a better climate. One such problem is stock market fraud. Like Elizabeth Warren, Guggenheim could investigate the Wall Street manipulations that sabotage Main Street's economy and its schools.

Another abuse that Guggenheim could explore is wage-theft. The students of *WFS* live in communities where parents are routinely robbed of wages by various illegal stratagems used by employers. Many of my own high-school students who work have been subjected to such "mugging by accounting" themselves.

Though the *WFS* students are themselves highly motivated, their disruptive classmates are extremely angry about their parents' low or missing wages and other examples of society's injustice. The alienated violence, both verbal and physical, perpetrated by such exploited students is the main reason why good students seek out charter schools.

A final problem from the list of many school-related evils that Guggenheim's Superman can't see is incarceration. The most alienated and disruptive students in school are those with parents, usually fathers, in jail. The highly profitable private-prison industry greatly enriches many in Guggenheim's social class but severely damages the public schools he professes to care about. The lack of vision here in Guggenheim's *Waiting for Superman* is obviously quite convenient.

In short, *Waiting for Superman* only sees the obvious *symptoms* of public school problems. It lacks the deeper vision of the superhero after which it is named. This should come as no surprise. If the DC Superman were employed in the service of a profiteering enterprise such as the charter school industry, those classic comics would have been written quite differently!

6. Thomas Putnam Meets Nietzsche

From the above, we can see that if Guggenheim were really interested in improving public schools rather than in merely promoting the charter school industry, he would direct his attention to the rich and powerful in his neighborhood.

However, like the blame-shifting medieval Inquisitors, *Guggenheim opts to prove his virtue by condemning others weaker than him.* Like Thomas Putnam of Salem, he also reaps a reward—definitely in film sales and perhaps in charter school investment—by accusing vulnerable women.

And yes, it is a sin to produce a witch-hunting indictment that helps to create such a hostile atmosphere that some teachers are driven to depression and at least one to his death. The absolution of one's guilt and the making of a profit (a masterful two-fer!) should not result in the death of others.

However, Guggenheim is responsible for more than creating a climate that contributed to the death of Rigoberto Ruelas Jr. The pen does indeed influence history itself. Nietzsche's *Zarathustra*, for example, helped to create the intellectual climate for Hitler's *Aryan Superman.*

Guggenheim has promoted the *Superman Complex*—the lust for a Superman savior to trample democratic procedures to get rid of insidious witches and get things done. This fascist longing has already had a political effect. Like Nietzsche, Guggenheim has helped to pave the way for one such self-proclaimed savior with superpowers—Donald Trump.

In paving the way for Trump and future political Superheroes who will trample democratic rights to "clean things up," Guggenheim has also helped to kill American democracy itself.

Myth #2: Teachers Don't Motivate

> *If students don't want to learn, isn't it because teachers aren't motivating them?*

This question will be thoroughly answered in *The Teacher's Manifesto II*. To briefly summarize here, kids are quite motivated when they are young. However, as they grow and become more acquainted with the highly unjust nature of American society, disadvantaged kids become alienated from it and lose their motivation for education.

Inner-city youth instead adopt the values of the peer group in their distressed neighborhood. Those values are naturally rebellious and rejecting of the larger society that has shunned the failing neighborhood.

In failing communities, student lack of motivation is not the passive, lazy inertia that some kids display in rich communities. In distressed communities, the lack of motivation is a determined, conscious choice. Kids just outright refuse to learn!

The resolute motivation to not learn is an active act of rebellion against the school—the most visible manifestation to the child of an institution of society. In sabotaging the school, whether by vandalism, classroom disruptions, or simply tuning out and failing, students subconsciously feel that they are getting back at the unjust society that has sabotaged their communities and families.

The angry alienation of exploited students has a devastating effect on teachers. Many good teachers simply leave the profession because of the emotional stress from being abused daily by students. Others stop trying as hard as they did when they were young in order to avoid continued student wrath. A few become bad teachers and do little in class.

Thus *Waiting for Superman* only got the second half of the story with regard to *some* teachers. Yes, there are indeed bad teachers in failing communities but they are only a few. More importantly, it wasn't teachers that created those communities.

Failing communities were created by slavery, discrimination, and exploitation. They are being perpetuated by the injustices of neoliberal capitalism and its accompanying austerity. The anger and violence in these communities create both alienated, disruptive students and a few bad teachers who simply give up.

Poor students today reject education and sabotage schools for exactly the same reason that the "possessed" kids of Salem disrupted church services. In both cases, the misbehavior occurs in a place where kids subconsciously feel they can safely vent their frustration about the insecurity and stresses of existence.

However, there is a fundamental difference between the two situations. The difference is that in 1692, the

Salem adults could do nothing to change the precariousness and harshness of life in the new land. Today, however, our adults can end the precariousness and harshness of life in failing communities by creating a more just society.

The lack of motivation of kids in failing communities is a therefore a *symptom* that indicates we need to seriously address the maladies of the larger society. Many problems in education are indeed mostly symptoms of those deeper maladies.

The people of Salem were poor, brought up in religious fanaticism, and lacked the self-knowledge that modern education can provide. Had they not suffered from those disadvantages, they would have willingly and easily addressed the deeper problems their kids faced.

Our society is rich and has all the advantages of sociological and psychological insight into the culture of poverty and the dysfunctional behavior it can produce. The only obstacle preventing us from addressing the real problems that afflict our kids is the devotion of our political and economic elite to fanatic, free-market neoliberalism. What would the adults of Salem have done with such leaders?

Unfortunately, our task is rather more difficult. We have to replace not leaders but the unjust economic system and the corrupt political arrangements that support it. Our kids from failing communities will become motivated when *we* demonstrate the motivation to change their conditions of life.

Myth #3:
Unions Are the Problem!

Aren't teachers unions the problem in education for protecting bad teachers and resisting much needed change?

It is true that teachers unions defend teachers accused of wrongdoing. That is one purpose of any union. Unlike police unions, however, teachers unions simply ensure that negotiated due process rights are respected. Moreover, the due process rights available to teachers are much fewer and weaker than those accorded to the police.

The concept of due process is an important human right that dates all the way back to the Magna Carta. It is true that due process will protect bad teachers—but *only until the process plays out.* This due process is the same principle of justice under which we do not lynch the accused—even if he is indeed guilty—but wait for a trial, with all the safeguards that this entails. Due process is thus a fundamental democratic right that ensures that citizens are protected from arbitrary punishment by those with power.

As with the legal system, due process in employment can be frustrating; however, to challenge the right to due process is to question one of the most ancient and fundamental aspects of democracy and justice. In education, after the due process has run its course, the teacher who has been proven to be deficient is quickly sanctioned or fired, unlike what happens in our police forces.

Teachers unions work to uphold standards in education. They actually help to maintain the quality of education by ensuring that teachers can grade fairly without being pressured to award undeserved passing grades to influential students such as athletes or the kids of powerful parents. Their protections allow conscientious teachers to teach important but controversial issues without reprisal.

Another way that teachers unions uphold standards is by questioning educational fads that are not based on serious, validated research. Unlike other professions in which changes are made on the basis on solid professional research, teaching is subject to the whims of those moved by *The Great Idea of the Month*. Such fads are often promoted by managers with little background in the field. In scientifically questioning changes based on the latest educational fashion, teachers unions are again standing up for the education of kids at the risk of angering educational profiteers who benefit from the promotion of such fads.

In addition, teachers unions help to maintain good learning environments in schools by insisting that administrators apply discipline standards that enable good students to learn without being distracted by disruptive students. If many school administrators had their way, disruptive students would be allowed to remain in the classroom to continue sabotaging education for everyone. This is because administrators—who are on the promotion track—don't want to deal with discipline (which is inherently controversial) and are afraid of parents complaining to the school board about their kids being punished. Administrators basically see discipline as a distraction from them proving to the higher authorities how innovative they are in educational management and in the promotion of the latest educational fad.

It is the teachers union which therefore protects not only the teacher but also the good students in the classroom by insisting that disruptive students receive the counseling and alternative education they need both for them to succeed and for good students to proceed with their education unmolested.

Strong teachers unions also prevent principals from behaving in bizarre ways that can harm student learning. When Principal Donna Connelly impetuously threw out *all* teachers' desks and filing cabinets at a Bronx school, it obviously greatly impeded instruction as teachers had no way to efficiently organize and access their materials to deliver instruction. A strong and effective teachers union would have inhibited Connelly from engaging in such outrageous behavior harmful to student learning.

It is precisely because teachers unions protect education from administrators with agendas other than learning that they are criticized. Had a strong union prevented Connelly from carrying out her maniacal dumping, this principal would have *condemned it for obstructionism!* Connelly is only a very extreme case of neoliberal principals drunk with power who make arbitrary decisions that hurt students. Teachers unions are thus regularly criticized when they point out flaws in similar harebrained policies and fads promoted by administrators on the promotion track eager to prove themselves.

As the ones who actually teach in the classroom, teachers have a sense of what would work, what would not be conducive to learning, and what would actually be disruptive. When a career dictatorial "Emergency Manager" such as Darnell Earley moves from poisoning Flint water to managing Detroit's public schools, *it is only the teachers union that stands in the way of his harming students and education* in the same manner he irreparably hurt Flint's children and residents.

The difference in the way neoliberal politicians and media pundits treat the input of mostly female teachers unions versus that of other male professional organizations is glaring. When males in professional organizations such as the American Medical Association contribute their expertise to the solution of problems in their profession, they are listened to and their recommendations are often adopted. It's quite the opposite in education. When female teachers in their professional organization—the teachers union—provide their input on changes, they are charged with obstructionism. Their union is then hounded like a witches' coven.

The obstructionist charge ignores the fact that *a healthy skepticism is the hallmark of science's reception to new ideas* and similarly the hallmark of any responsible professional organization employing scientific standards. As such an organization, the teachers union is obstructionist only in the sense that it believes changes should be based on solid research not the feel-good motivational idea of the month. *The teachers union also opposes educational changes based on the same type of neoliberal values that poisoned the kids of Flint, Michigan.*

In conclusion, teachers unions, like other employee associations, may indeed temporarily protect a bad worker until her due process—a fundamental democratic right—has been completed. However, the temporary harm this causes is vastly outweighed by the many ways teachers unions maintain solid educational standards, defend professional standards, promote good learning environments, and defend the rights of students to learn free from fads and exploitative neoliberal "reform" practices.

CHAPTER 14

───── ❧ ─────

Liberal Betrayal and Trump's Rise

THE RISE OF Donald Trump is a jarring indication of the failure of liberalism. Political liberalism (no connection to economic neoliberalism) seeks to humanize capitalism with reforms. It was once successful but its present willing subordination to corporate interests has created the discontent that is now exploited by Trump.

Political liberalism had a brief period of success in the West when communism posed an alternative and the West dominated the world's capitalist system. The threat of a communist alternative and the economic dominance of the world both impelled and enabled Western governments to provide social services and pensions for their citizens, while enabling upward mobility with low-cost higher education. With the communist alternative gone and the economic dominance ended, fundamentalist free-market capitalism has returned to the West with a vengeance in the form of neoliberalism and austerity.

Western liberals have now adopted the free-market neoliberalism propounded by their conservative opponents. They have had to do so because corporate interests dominate the electoral process, especially in the United

States. Political liberalism has thus been left to differentiate itself from conservativism merely on *social* issues like gay marriage and women's access to abortions.

The economic injustice now ignored by political liberalism festers from neglect. Unrestrained by government, neoliberal capitalism reduces the standard of living of the average citizen and makes his job insecure. It threatens his pension, his Social Security, his water, and his very health. It is little wonder, therefore, that much of the population is seething with anger.

The anger can be directed in two very different ways. It can be focused where it is justified—at the powerful economic interests and their political servants who have created economic injustice. This is precisely what Bernie Sanders is doing in advocating for radical structural change. The corporate media, however, marginalizes Bernie and his ideas because he is a socialist.

Citizens' anger can also be exploited by demagogues. This is exactly what Trump is doing. In manipulating such anger, Trump has exploited the *Superman Complex* that liberals themselves have promoted. The *Superman Complex*, remember, is the undemocratic wish for a strongman to come in, take charge, and clear up the mess—in education, in the economy, and elsewhere.

In promoting witch-hunting and the fascist *Superman Complex* in his film *Waiting for Superman*, the wealthy producer Davis Guggenheim has helped to create public acceptance for his fellow-billionaire Superman to emerge.

This Superman will *make America great again* by finding new witches to burn.

More importantly, in accepting rather than opposing neoliberal capitalism, liberals have joined conservatives in creating a more unequal and unjust society rife with social problems. Like conservatives, they have then shifted the blame for these problems onto teachers and public schools. Indeed, liberals have sometimes been more vitriolic in attacking teachers precisely because they do care, to some extent, for the poor.

The scapegoating of teachers presaged Trump's scapegoating of minorities and prepared the way for it. When Trump engages in one of his witch-hunting tantrums, we understand that it is a result of his unstable personality. Similarly, when liberals scapegoat teachers, it actually reveals as much about their psyches as Trump's tirades do about him.

Two of the most famous liberal promoters of charter schools and critics of public school teachers are Obama and Bill Gates. Their unfair criticisms do not stem from a reasoned and factual critique of the public school system or of teachers unions. Instead, the criticisms made by Obama and Gates originate from *powerful emotional issues stemming from their backgrounds which they project onto teachers and the public school system today.*

In brief, Obama and Gates have hang-ups from their childhoods which they try to resolve by blaming teachers. These personal agendas dovetail neatly with their need to find scapegoats for the problems caused by the system that enriches them and enables their celebrity.

Obama: The Missing Dad Syndrome

The courts have long considered schools and teachers to be *in loco parentis*, i.e., schools assume the authority of the *parent* in a situation where the parent cannot be present. As someone who has taught both in the USA and abroad for over twenty years, I can vouch that students in many cultures as well as the United States do indeed see teachers as parental-type figures. My colleagues have also found the same to be true. Indeed, teachers sometimes have to reluctantly draw a line with those emotionally needy students who want them to function more as a parent than a teacher.

The emotionally needy student who tends to see the teacher as more of a parent than a teacher is generally *the student from a single-parent family*. With that family background, the student sees the teacher as the missing parent, whether as the mother or the father. The parent at home may be the best parent ever, but the child from a single-parent family will still have emotional needs unmet. This is especially the case when the other parent has totally disappeared from the child's life. In that situation, the student will often want his or her emotional needs as a child to be fulfilled by teachers.

Obama's father disappeared from his son's life. *This missing father was an academic, which is what teachers are.*

In his book, *Dreams from My Father*, Obama describes being motivated by his father's social conscience during his youth and tells of seeking out mentors and teachers who happened to have similar political perspectives. Although *Dreams from My Father* is indeed a dreamy tribute to Obama's father, it is precisely dreamy because the father is missing. So what is the flipside to this public dreamy idealization? What is happening at the subconscious level that may be neither so dreamy nor so full of admiration?

The flipside to Obama's early wistful idealization of his father is hinted at in his notoriously guarded emotions today. We know that when a parent abandons a child, *it creates anger in that child*. Unexpressed and unresolved anger about abandonment results in guarded emotions. It therefore takes no stretch of the imagination to see that Obama is emotionally guarded because his father abandoned him. However, anger and disappointment that is suppressed must still somehow find an outlet. The target for this anger of abandonment will be the person or group *who most closely resembles the original but unpunished culprit* responsible for the disappointment and anger.

Enter teachers! In *Dreams from My Father*, Obama approvingly tells of teachers with social consciences who during his youth carried on the *positive* values of his father for him. But the *negative* values? Who will be identified as carrying on the *uncaring, irresponsible behavior of the father* as Obama's suppressed anger about abandonment ripens with age and later comes to the surface?

In a situation where Obama himself identifies teachers who carry on the positive values of his father, and where Obama also has private negative resentments against his father, it is obvious that Obama will also *identify teachers with the negative behavior of his father,* particularly the act of **abandonment.**

Basically, Obama is accusing teachers of abandoning their duty to the young because he was himself abandoned by his father as a child! The similarities between Obama's legitimate grievances against his father and Obama's negative attitudes to teachers are indeed eerie. The coldness that Obama displayed to the Central Falls teachers was the coldness that he was reciprocating to his father image for being abandoned. This misplaced coldness, however, helped to drive Rigoberto Ruelas Jr. to his death.

Proof that Obama's own pain of abandonment is triggered by the apparent abandonment of kids today lies in his key January 2016 speech on gun control. The normally emotionally-repressed Obama actually cried! Donald Trump claimed that Obama faked the tears with onions, but the weeping was real enough. It was caused by the images of vulnerable kids at school hurt without a parent to comfort them, a hurt that revived Obama's own lingering childhood trauma of abandonment. For Obama, the problem was not just that the Sandy Hook kids had been killed but that they had actually been *abandoned* to such violence by US negligence on gun control—the issue about which he so passionately spoke that day.

Obama is certainly right that America has abandoned its kids to guns. However, it is similarly America—and not its teachers—that has abandoned its poor kids to failing communities, an abandonment that sabotages their education. Obama fails to recognize this because his acceptance of neoliberal capitalism—the cause of poverty—trumps his genuine concern for America's kids.

In a situation where American capitalism is actually failing America's children, Obama's loyalty to the former and his continued sense of childhood abandonment combine to create a cold and cruel witch-hunting displacement: *It is obviously teachers who are the ones abandoning America's school kids!*

Gates: Mongol Emperor of Education

A second famous critic of public school education is Bill Gates. Unlike Obama, he grew up very privileged, in a white upper middle-class family. Gates' antipathy towards public high schools derives from his own privileged private school experiences.

Gates initially attended a public school. However, his parents noticed that he seemed bored and withdrawn, attributing this to his not being challenged at school. They therefore enrolled him at the age of thirteen in Lakeside School, an exclusive private preparatory school with a small student-to-teacher ratio and state-of-the-art equipment and facilities. This was all funded by the school's high tuition and donations from the upper middle-class parents.

Gates blossomed at this well-funded school, citing the *close relationships* he developed with teachers and the *freedom* he had to pursue his love—computers. (He was excused from math class to study computers!) It was at Lakeside that Gates met Paul Allen, with whom he bonded over computers and formed his first computer company.

In the "reforms" he now pushes on public education, Gates seems to have forgotten what he loved about his private school experiences! Gates is asking good teachers to *take on five more students* per class for extra pay. With classroom size already high in public schools, this would totally eliminate the ability of public school teachers to develop the close relationship with students that Gates experienced at his private school. It also ignores the commonsense knowledge of what large classrooms do to teaching effectiveness. In economics, this is known as the law of diminishing returns.

Moreover, the testing regimen for students that Gates endorses to evaluate teachers *destroys for students any semblance of the freedom that Gates himself had* in his ability to pursue his academic love during class time. In this era of testing mania, teachers cannot allow students to study outside of their subject area because both teachers and schools are being evaluated on students' test scores.

The billionaire entrepreneur Gates seems to believe that Lakeside's secret lay simply in it being non-public rather than it being well-funded, well-equipped, and free from rigid oversight. Gates' attitude to public schools and its teachers is the dismissive disdain, distrust, and blame the wealthy express towards the institutions serving the common people—even as they express concern about the problems the latter face.

Thus, instead of pushing for public schools to be *funded, equipped, and pedagogically free* to the same extent that Lakeside School was, Gates pushes for more charter schools. Gates' belief in the innate superiority of a non-public school is an ideological one, part of the secular religion of the American free-enterprise capitalism that so greatly enriches him. (As with other fundamentalist religions, this neoliberal ideology is harming the country that generates it, a phenomenon we will explore further in *The Teacher's Manifesto II*.)

Gates suffers from the same clueless, privileged liberal guilt as Davis Guggenheim (the producer of *Waiting for Superman*) that causes him to likewise idealize inner-city public school students. Like Guggenheim, he has no concept of the alienation in failing communities. He has no idea of the roughness in public schools that results from this alienation. Thus, Gates also has the sheltered liberal's naive image of the noble poor. This image ignores the dysfunctions that poverty creates in distressed communities, dysfunctions that are inevitably brought to public schools by the poor kids of those communities.

Gates believes poor students could and would escape their poverty if they were not failed by unresponsive public schools. In his narcissistic thinking, he mistakenly assumes that kids in inner cities are turned off from their public school education for the same reason that he was. *Gates confuses his own jaded lack of motivation as a bored, brilliant, rich white kid with the far more serious angry rebellious rejection of motivation by poor and minority youth savaged by capitalist society and the effects of racism.*

Gates fails to realize that kids traumatized by poverty today reject education and act up in school for precisely the same reason that the "possessed" Salem kids acted up during church services—to seek release from the stresses of life.

Gates' linking of his own boredom with this active shunning of education by inner city youth is a patronizing attempt to identify with the exploited, an act of intellectual "slumming." Gates' exclusion of Caucasian students from his generous Millennium scholarships similarly shows his attempt to identify with minorities, ignoring the fact that many whites are similarly impoverished and exploited. His disregard for the plight of working-class whites makes them resentful and drives some into the arms of Donald Trump. This divides the working class.

The wonderful musical, *Fiddler on the Roof*, sheds light on Gates' attitude to his fantastic wealth. In its iconic song "If I Were A Rich Man," the lead character Tevye wistfully muses about how wealth would change his life for the better. He declares with imagined pride:

If I were a rich man...
The most important men in town
Will come to fawn on me.
They will ask me to advise them,

Like a Solomon the Wise,
Posing problems that would cross a Rabbi's eyes.
And it won't make one bit of difference
If I answer right or wrong.
<u>*When you're rich, they think you really know*</u>*!*

Unlike Tevye, Gates doesn't have to imagine; he is rich. Gates is therefore able to act out Tevye's fantasy of commanding attention for expounding on problems about which he knows little. Unlike the simple but honest Tevye, Gates refuses to acknowledge that he just doesn't "know."

Gates commits one of the fundamental errors in human thinking: confusing one's own experience with an issue with the far different experiences faced by others. Gates doesn't realize that one's personal background is not always the fount of wisdom from which to solve larger and unrelated social problems.

Unlike Tevye's imagined "rich man's" pronouncements, Gates' declarations do make a difference. He uses his wealth to push for rigid and damaging policies for public schools, e.g., relentless testing and instruction geared around it. The tragic irony is that such policies are *in direct opposition to what Gates loved* about his privileged private preparatory school!

Nowhere, of course, does the billionaire Gates advocate for dramatically reforming the capitalist system to eliminate the militantly resistant alienation that sabotages public schools in failing communities. Like Guggenheim, Gates refuses to recognize this alienation and its source.

Having idealized inner-city students, many of whom basically suffer from a form of PTSD caused by chronic poverty, Gates then transfers the blame for the collateral damage that capitalism inflicts. Capitalist society is absolved of the evil of creating such dystopias as failing communities. The fault is instead assigned to the public institution—the school—mandated the impossible task of undoing capitalism's damage.

Gates shuns working for the fundamental economic reform that would eliminate both failing communities and their consequential "failing schools." Instead, he finds it much more rewarding to continue to earn phenomenally from the exploitative capitalist system that grossly underpays the parents of the students in those schools.

With his wealth that is essentially exploited from the parents of the students about whom he cares, Gates can easily build a 66,000 square foot home worth $154 million. The technological wizardry in this home creates a fantasyland of power. Having his every private whim satisfied in his dream caste, Gates then finds it similarly much more rewarding psychologically to receive praise for donating some of his earnings to reshape the world according to his ideological whims.

In a democratic society, public education would be democratically funded through adequate taxes on people like Gates, with policies then determined democratically by professionals and the citizenry. Instead, public education is starved, made dependent on donors like Gates, and then drastically scarred by the private ideological "reforms" such donors impose as conditions of their Trojan horse "gifts."

The point is that *Gates' narcissistic philanthropy would be unnecessary if he instead worked to create a more just society*—one in which the money for self-indulgent mega-mega-mansions would instead go to schools. Such a society would reduce the alienation of poor students about inequality, economic injustice, and poverty, making them more receptive to education.

This phenomenon of the rich using their immense economic power to reshape society according to their whims is a growing hobby of the privileged in our increasingly unequal country. It is a way for them to *alleviate their consciences for benefitting from the injustices that hurt those about whom they supposedly care.*

Socially, the increase in the number of such supposedly selfless benefactors heralds the return to a system of feudalistic patronage in which the poor and powerless are dependent on the goodwill of the rich. Such a society is that which characterized Latin America a century ago (with *peons* depending on the *patron*) and such a society is that to which our growing inequality is taking us.

Union busting and neoliberal austerity are taking away the dignity and independence of the American worker and professional. Such dignity was formerly guaranteed by union contracts that spelled out good wages, secure benefits, and workplace rights as well as by social democratic benefits paid for by taxes on the people of Gates' socioeconomic class. The independence of the American worker, professional, and citizen is now being replaced by their becoming cravenly dependent on the goodwill of the employer and the largesse of a benefactor like Bill Gates.

If there is any doubt about the intentions of such benefactors to subvert democracy and human rights, it should be dispelled by the name of Gates' $154 million castle and fiefdom—*Xanadu*. Xanadu was the summer palace of the fabulously wealthy and immensely powerful Mongol-Chinese emperor Kublai Khan. This fabulous summer palace in Mongolia and the dreadful power of its owner inspired Coleridge's classic poem *Kubla Khan*.

In order to be fabulously wealthy, the Mongol Empire was the cruelest ever in the history of the world. In its discarding of people at home and abroad, neoliberalism carries on this Mongol tradition—including in education, in the poisoning of Flint's water supply, and in the denial of their own water to the people of Bolivia. The naming of the home of America's most famous neoliberal "reformer" is thus no accident; it reveals the sort of society that he and his social class want to create.

As America devolves into an economic feudalism controlled by various mega-billionaires, Bill Gates acts like the Latin *patron* of old; he has to find someone else to blame for the misery of his *peon*. Thus, like the similarly fabulously wealthy Guggenheim, Gates finds the easiest solution for this crisis of conscience. He scapegoats "incompetent teachers" for the non-performance of students rendered resolutely unmotivated by the blows of poverty that stun their consciousness.

If Gates truly cared about poverty rather than about his charity empire and legacy, he would instead advocate for radical social reform. Like the similarly fabulously wealthy Warren Buffet, he would advocate for much higher taxes on the rich like himself.

If Gates were really serious about helping poor students, he would support the reforms proposed by Bernie Sanders and Jill Stein of the Green Party. Such economic justice would fund both better schools and radically improved neighborhoods. These are the real reforms that would eliminate the angry alienation of youth in America's failing communities that sabotages American education.

Until Gates commits to such fundamental reform, the best advice on how to deal with him comes from Samuel Taylor Coleridge. Coleridge cautions us about wealth and power in the last lines of his poem about Xanadu and Gates' terrible mentor, Kublai Khan. Coleridge specifically warns mere mortals about the danger of being dazzled by he who carves out his earthly paradise of Xanadu at the expense of others:

> *And all should cry, **Beware! Beware!***
> *His flashing eyes, his floating hair!*
> *Weave a circle round him thrice,*
> *And close your eyes with holy dread,*
> *For he on honey-dew hath fed,*
> *And drunk the milk of Paradise.*

The original Kublai Khan was drunk with power in his Mongolian paradise of Xanadu. Our Kublai Khan of today is similarly besotten with power in his modern Xanadu—one that would put Kublai's to shame. Coleridge knew that drinking "the milk of Paradise"—i.e., accumulating extreme wealth and power—destroyed the soul. His advice to be wary of Kublai and his power-lust is advice that we ignore at our peril.

Discipline, Charters, and Superman

The violent behavior some students exhibit in public school cafeterias across the nation (see the last section in Chapter Eleven) also occurs in hallways and the classroom itself. Privileged liberals who have attended private school and live ensconced in their fabulous *Xanadus* are totally clueless about such dangerous and disruptive student conduct. However, this behavior and its effect on student learning is the principal reason why *serious or scared students will opt for the charter school* over the traditional public school.

The charter has the option of rejecting dangerous students. In contrast, the traditional public school has to let all students attend. When some disrupt the school or the classroom itself, the school is sometimes hamstrung by politically correct disciplinary measures that derive from community pressure. Such pressure gains liberal support. *This politically correct pressure permits the continued disruption of the classroom.*

Politically correct liberals in authority find it easier to blame teachers for classroom problems rather than to summon the courage to point to the natural resentment and anger of those whose families are physically and psychologically damaged by capitalist injustice. Having severely *weakened public schools* with politically-correct, lax discipline, liberals then further sabotage them by promoting charter schools that *suck out the best students* from the dangerous public schools they have helped to create.

This issue of discipline is an extremely difficult one. The community pressure defending disruptive disadvantaged students is understandable given the injustice that those in failing communities face. Moreover, the solution to America's school discipline problem most certainly does *not* lie in fascistic-type discipline. However, the lax politically-correct indulgence that exists now similarly fails to address the deeper, common problems behind student misbehavior. Tolerating student misbehavior also leads to chaos in the schools, which drives some frustrated teachers and parents into the arms of Donald Trump.

Discipline is simply *not* an individual issue. The epidemic of disruptive behavior by students is as much a symptom of underlying social problems in failing communities as is the epidemic of crime in those selfsame communities. Discipline must therefore be accompanied by intensive counseling and therapy as well as by society's commitment to *fundamentally change the conditions in the student's community* that produce such alienated, nihilistic disruption.

The true synthesis of the liberal and conservative attitudes on discipline is thus a radical one—one that gets to the root of the problem:

- Well-behaved students must be allowed to learn without being intimidated or having their classrooms disrupted by their more troubled classmates. Allowing focused, disadvantaged students to have their education sabotaged by their more emotionally vulnerable classmates is just one more injustice inflicted on them.

- Teachers must be allowed to teach without being verbally or physically abused by highly troubled students. The sexism that permits such daily abuse of teachers must be pointed out and addressed. Note well that this is a sexism that is practiced far more by liberals than by conservatives.

- Most disruptive students must be viewed *not* as enforcement issues. Chronic and widespread disruption must instead be addressed as *symptoms of the therapy needed* to undo the psychological damage caused by capitalist injustice.

- More fundamentally, chronic anti-social behavior in schools must be seen as indicators of the need for *radical neighborhood uplift*. Just as special funds are allocated to the police and military to deal with emergencies, so should funding be directed to the rehabilitation and reorganization of failing communities.

- New funding for schools and failing communities must be obtained by higher taxes on Bill Gates, Barack Obama, Davis Guggenheim, and others of their class. This would dramatically improve the living conditions for disadvantaged students and hence increase their emotional stability and psychological school readiness.

The vexing issue of discipline will be explored further in *The Teacher's Manifesto II*. For now, there is one final thing to note about the news reports of fighting in the cafeterias and general violence in the schools. In its portrayal of public schools, *Waiting for Superman (WFS)* does *not* depict any such violent or even merely disruptive students. Only their very angelic opposites are featured.

Why is *WFS*, a supposedly ground-breaking movie, so selective when its declared goal is to examine public education? It's simple. Depicting the reality of such violent or disruptive students would ruin the film's witch-hunting agenda set by its billionaire liberal producer, Davis Guggenheim. This guilt-shifting agenda allows him to keep his billions while blaming teachers for the inequality that turns some American schools into war zones.

The Failure of Liberalism and the Rise of Trumpism

Liberal leaders and thinkers such as Obama, Gates, Guggenheim, and the Clintons have failed not only teachers but also the struggle for justice itself. They prefer to become *highly compensated celebrities within the world of neoliberal capitalism* rather than to lead the struggle to fundamentally change that system.

Liberals thrive—emotionally and materially—on praise and patronage for opposing some of the excesses of neoliberalism or ameliorating some of its inevitably destructive side effects. However, in the end, they facilitate neoliberalism and its inherent exploitation. This is why political liberals follow neoliberal conservatives and scapegoat teachers for the problems of capitalism—whether it be poor student discipline, low student achievement, or poverty itself.

Liberals politicians like Obama and the Clintons and liberal activists like Guggenheim and Gates find it financially and morally convenient to blame the education workers for problems created by the capitalist system that enriches them and enables their celebrity. In doing so, they have let Donald Trump exploit the problems they ignore and also paved the way for Trumpism—the mass scapegoating we see at Trump's rallies.

Teachers and others fighting for justice therefore cannot place their hope for fundamental relief and reform on a liberal leader or on Trump. Instead, they must get to the root of the problem by *making alliances—at home and abroad—with others who are also exploited by neoliberal capitalism*. Freedom from our individual exploitation lies in the unity of *all* workers, professionals, and consumers, wherever they may be.

CHAPTER 15

Making Sense of Absurdity

KAFKA WROTE ABOUT the absurdities of modern life, something that American teachers would appreciate when they are called in to be interrogated about the results of the modern-day witch tests. However, absurdities are also inflicted on other workers and professionals in America. It is the chaos and resentment created by such absurdities that lead to the emergence of absurd but dangerous demagogues like Donald Trump.

Unjust absurdities are afflicting the entire world. One outrageous instance was when Bolivians could not collect rainwater from their rooftops and streams because a foreign company owned their water system. Another befell the people of Flint, Michigan when they were poisoned by their venture capitalist governor through austerity cuts implemented with the goal of privatization. It is the pitiless force of neoliberal capitalism that generates these absurdities at home and all around the globe in order to enrich the few at the expense of the many.

In getting to the root of the witch hunts against teachers in America, _The Teacher's Manifesto_ has therefore ranged over many diverse topics, relating them all to problems in education and attacks on teachers. Here is a synthesis of how all these issues are connected and an expansion on the synthesis that enables us to go beyond Kafka and make some sense of these absurdities in order to effectively overcome them. Some of the new connections made below will be more fully developed in *The Teacher's Manifesto II*.

Scapegoating occurs in societies that are demoralized and feel threatened. America's Puritan heritage makes the country particularly susceptible to such witch hunts. The Puritan ideology, with its concept of the world being a battleground of good and evil, leads those who continually seek to cleanse society of wrongdoers to search for hidden enemies engaged in subterfuge. In so doing, these witch hunters blindly and viciously attack those who are innocent but vulnerable. Being vulnerable, women in America have been the victim of witch hunts since the Salem witch trials.

Problems in American education exist not in wealthy communities but in failing ones beset by poverty, neglect, and alienation. This clearly shows that economic injustice, not bad teachers, is the root problem in education. This fact has been confirmed by extensive documentation in both investigative news reporting and academic research. Blaming the mostly female, feminine-type profession of teaching for the problems of schools in failing communities is thus part of the scapegoating tradition of blaming innocent, vulnerable women for society's ills. The hounding of American teachers is therefore merely a repeat of the injustice of Salem, Massachusetts in 1692.

Just as many accusers in Salem had motives of material gain, so do those who attack teachers and public education today. Their goal is to discredit public education and to make the system so dysfunctional with onerous testing and monitoring that parents turn to charter and private schools. This provides a new source of revenue for capitalist investment. For-profit educational enterprises therefore donate heavily to the politicians who both attack public schools and promote the alternatives that benefit these education profiteers.

However, educational privatization has failed where it has been tried most fully. The horrible failure of educational privatization in Chile is a warning to us not to follow that path here. At home, a similar warning exists in the outrageous abuses perpetrated in Florida by for-profit schools at both the college and K–12 levels.

Teachers in public education are not the only ones under attack. The movement to privatize many such government entities is called *neoliberalism*, which seeks to bring back *the unrestricted, laissez-faire capitalism* of the late 1800s. Neoliberalism consequently dismantles the New Deal and social-democratic reforms of the United States and Europe—the very reforms that expanded the middle class! As neoliberalism is successful in bringing back laissez faire capitalism, it squeezes the working and professional classes in America and Europe.

Neoliberalism does its greatest harm to the countries of the "Third World" which were exploited as colonies to enrich the West. Capitalism was only able to develop in the West because the latter (1) expropriated Native American land and precious metals; (2) enslaved Africans to get free labor; and (3) forcibly controlled the thriving Asian trade.

Neoliberalism, which claims the goal of bringing back "free-market capitalism," is thus *based on a lie* because the success of capitalism has always depended on the subjugation of the people of three continents. This history of capitalism requiring subjugation—both external and internal—is extremely important in understanding both *foreign wars* and the current *domestic war on the public sphere*, including education.

The history of capitalism is also important in specifically evaluating the call for privatization in American education. A closer look at the actual relevant history clearly disproves the claim that laissez-faire in the economy benefits everyone. Administrations that followed laissez-faire in America have always created the conditions for economic collapse, as in the 1890s, the 1920s, and the 2000s. Neoliberalism's attempt to bring back laissez-faire by imposing it first on education is similarly leading to educational collapse in America.

Abroad, neoliberalism continues subjugation not with outright empires but by spawning regime change and wars in order to maintain control of resources and markets in the Global South (the countries that used to be called the Third World). The United States helped to impose a neoliberal dictatorship in Chile which implemented the same neoliberal "reforms," including educational "choice," that are currently being promoted here. However, Chile is now trying to undo the devastating damage that the educational free market wrought on the country's education system.

Neoliberal capitalism endangers professionalism and democracy itself. The rights of the people have to be curtailed in order to forcibly implement unpopular austerity cuts and privatization. Chile's experience with neoliberal dictatorship was just a dry run for what is now being forcibly implemented piecemeal in the West as workers and professionals lose rights.

Neoliberal capitalism has also supported Islamic fanatics in order to destroy any chance of modern, socialist reform in parts of the Global South. In doing so, it has destroyed secular education, freedom of religion, and the rights of women in many Muslim-majority countries. In its effort to control resources, neoliberalism has turned some of these lands into war-ravaged, nightmares of hell overrun by bloodthirsty religious psychopaths. When the chaos spreads uncontrollably, Western neoliberal politicians express shock that the murderous fanatics have savagely turned on them.

When the profits of neoliberal capitalism are threatened abroad, the wealthy classes in the West turn the screws on workers and professionals at home in order to extract more profits here. The attack on public education is merely an attempt to discredit that field and then privatize it to provide a new source of revenue for capitalist investment at home.

In the attack on public education, *the rights of students, teachers, parents, and school districts are being curtailed* in order to promote the enterprises of educational profiteers. ***The freedom of those who control the market is replacing the freedom of communities to organize their education and provide decently for it.*** The freedom of wealthy corporations and individuals to bank offshore and avoid the taxes that would help schools has already replaced the fundamental right of children to have a decent education.

As happened earlier with American workers, American professionals including teachers are being subjected to declining pay and worsening conditions of work, including the loss of fundamental democratic rights. Professionals who are not being hurt are the officers in the uniformed services, such as cops. One important reason for this double standard of tolerating police non-performance and misconduct while unfairly blaming teachers is this old human trait: *sexism.*

Militarized institutions such as the police also help to preserve the inherent unfairness of the system by suppressing criminal and political reactions to it. Gross inequality therefore requires some to be ***enforcers*** and privileged beneficiaries of injustice and others to be ***scapegoats*** for its effects on the poor.

The fundamental injustice of capitalism thus explains the outrageous but symbiotic disparity in the treatment of cops and teachers—our enforcers and our scapegoats. The latter role is just as important to capitalism as the former.

The demonization of teachers thus results from a horrible synthesis of *five virulent tendencies:*

1. *Sexism*—manifest in contempt for the mostly female, feminine-type profession of education
2. *Puritan Fanaticism*—manifest in scapegoating those who are vulnerable and in promoting religious schools and religious-influenced charters at the expense of secular public schools.
3. *Capitalist Opportunism*—manifest in the targeting for privatization those vulnerable schools in failing communities betrayed by capitalism and its politicians.
4. *Neoliberal Ideology*—manifest in the proclamation of catchy free-market slogans that sound attractive but which severely disappoint when privatization is actually implemented.
5. *Liberal Betrayal*—manifest in failing to get to the root of the problems facing poor and minority youth in America and in savagely blaming teachers instead.

Neoliberalism preaches austerity and enacts budget cuts so that the middle-class and the poor have to make sacrifices in order to further enrich the wealthy who want their taxes cut. These budget cuts have actually resulted in the deaths and poisoning of many of our children. In doing so, neoliberalism is merely the latest in a line of fanatical ideologies throughout history that have sacrificed people for an idea.

With its dogmatic, heartless laissez-faire ideology, neoliberal capitalism's relentless war against people has all the trappings of a *jihad*—and is just as deadly, only in more indirect ways. In this ideological and economic war, neoliberalism is immiserating the working class around the world and destroying the professional class in America and Europe.

As we have noted, neoliberalism has worked hand in hand with Islamic jihadists in Afghanistan, Iraq, Syria, and Libya. Apart from poisoning water and food at home, neoliberalism's own jihad includes petty Kafka-like absurdities such as preventing American teachers from going to the teachers' lounge and throwing out teachers' desks and filing cabinets. More seriously, neoliberal capitalism threatens the very survival of our species and planet with climate change due to its inexorable need to expand the economy and profits.

So, why is the situation for teachers so bad now and why wasn't it like that before? Answering this question will help us find a permanent solution to the scapegoating that teachers face today. Here is the answer to this puzzle:

- *Crisis:* Western capitalism only tolerated increased benefits for labor (including professional labor) from the 1950s to the 1970s because of the alternative posed by Communism and because of dominance of the international economy. With both gone, neoliberal capitalism is now demanding "*givebacks*" and simply will not allow a return to that relatively benign period of sharing between the classes in the West.

- *Blame Shifting:* Givebacks and government cutbacks drastically reduce people's standard of living. They create discontent. Politicians need to find a *scapegoat* for the problem of decaying living conditions and resultant student alienation. Teachers, being mostly female, are a convenient target.
- *Destroying the Opposition:* Scapegoating destroys teachers unions, thereby eliminating the main opposition to opening up education to profit-making vulture investment.
- *Religious Politics:* Religious leaders—active in politics since the 1980s—promote charter schools in order to have access to public funds, sometimes simply to embezzle and always to implement a religious agenda in schools they can control.

Political liberalism—as exemplified by Obama and the Clintons—merely seeks to smooth out the roughest edges of neoliberal capitalism. Operating as part of neoliberalism, liberals like Obama have been just as bad as conservatives in hounding teachers because they are afraid to go to the root of the problem—poverty and economic injustice. In failing to address the fundamental problems inherent in neoliberal capitalism, liberals have created the opportunity for demagogues like Donald Trump to emerge.

To solve the problems caused by neoliberalism—whether they be the scapegoating of teachers, declining pay and working conditions for all workers, police abuses, or the poisoning of citizens—we must therefore go step by step *beyond neoliberal capitalism and the traditional mainstream American political ideologies* that perpetuate it.

CHAPTER 16

—— ❧ ——

From Absurdity to Justice

The worst illiterate is the political illiterate: he doesn't hear, doesn't speak, nor participates in the political events. He doesn't know the cost of life, the price of the bean, of the fish, of the flour, of the rent, of the shoes and of the medicine, all depends on political decisions.

The political illiterate is so stupid that he is proud and swells his chest saying that he hates politics. The imbecile doesn't know that, <u>from his political ignorance is born the prostitute, the abandoned child, and the worst thieves of all</u>, the bad politician, corrupted and flunky of the national and multinational companies.

BERTOLT BRECHT

To STOP THE demonization of teachers and undo other injustices of neoliberal capitalism, we must get to the very root of the problem. We therefore have to *go beyond political liberalism*. We cannot just focus on our own issues, for this will lead to repeated defeat in such isolated struggles. To effectively resist, we must thus unite with others victimized by neoliberalism, give up our treasured nationalistic-type patriotism that supports neoliberalism abroad, and *attack neoliberal capitalism itself.*

Neoliberalism and American exceptionalism have to be *replaced with a democratic economy and a human patriotism* which puts workers and professionals first and which is compatible with respect for others on the planet and for the planet itself. A commitment to improving education therefore requires *activism* with both a local focus and international perspective. It requires *solidarity*, geared to ending the exploitation of neoliberal capitalism wherever it manifests itself.

This is what we would do: at home, we struggle for **economic justice**, which includes adequate support for education. Parents in Chicago have started doing this with demonstrations and sit-ins. Chicago teachers have even gone on strike.

We demand parity between professions of different gender: just as more police and resources are directed to high-crime, failing communities, so should more teachers and resources be allocated to the same high-dropout, failing neighborhoods.

In the course of supporting education, we also *change the very economic structure of inequality* that causes the basic problem in education—poverty. We restore tax rates to what they were under Eisenhower, with a top rate on the super-rich of 90%. We tax Wall Street transactions. We cooperate with international organizations to eliminate offshore banking.

We then use the taxes that the rich have been avoiding to properly fund public schools. We turn schools into comprehensive community centers. These would provide the basic support—medical, counseling, tutoring, and meals—that families need in order for their children to succeed educationally.

We also support our adult citizens. We subsidize state universities so that state residents can attend for just a nominal charge. We both eliminate the complexity and cost of Obamacare by enrolling all Americans in Medicare and also institute controls on the cost of drugs. To ensure that working people can survive, we implement a $15 minimum wage.

Basically, we ensure that the rich help to solve the problems created by the system that enriches them. In the course of making these reforms, we even consider ***fundamental structural changes*** that alter the relationship between owners and workers and between managers and employees.

In politics, we *remove the influence of money* by publically financing elections with specific taxes on speculative Wall Street transactions. Wall Street already pays to influence elections; this change ensures that they continue paying but without any such influence! We revoke the Citizens United decision and prohibit corporate campaign contributions of any sort. We *outlaw the revolving door* of politicians becoming corporate heads, lobbyists, etc. in which representatives legislate for their future employers rather than their current constituents.

Abroad, *we oppose wars* that are waged both to divert our attention from domestic struggles and also to unfairly secure access to other people's resources. (Yes, Islamic fanaticism is a serious problem that must be countered. However, in doing so, we must remember that (1) it became a worldwide problem because it was cultivated by Western political and economic elites and (2) Western wars to control resources perpetuate this violent extremism. The best solution to Islamic fanaticism is to support socialist governments in the Muslim world that will both promote secularism and ensure that the basic needs of people are met. This will ensure that fanaticism remains confined to an isolated and discredited minority, as it was in the 1960s and early 1970s before Western support for jihadists enabled them to multiply.)

In reducing our war making, we also drastically *cut down the size of the military* and use the savings for domestic concerns like education. We eliminate the odious power that Eisenhower warned about—the enormous influence of the military-industrial complex. Such power has grown considerably since his time and is seen in the instigation of needless conflicts such the 2003 Iraq War. To save the lives of our young, our national treasure, and our reputation abroad, we therefore *nationalize defense industries.*

Step by step, as we are successful in rolling back neo-liberal capitalism at home and abroad and changing the corrupt political systems that perpetuate it, new patterns of economic arrangements, political representation, and political participation will appear. The common theme in both economics and politics will be a ***real democracy*** that serves the people because it is not controlled by the private interests of those with enormous accumulated wealth.

*There is no blueprint; the continual struggle for justice—**a justice for all**—is the means that will reveal the ever-evolving goal.*

The first step is to liberate our minds. In *Amusing Ourselves to Death*, Neil Postman, building on Aldous Huxley's *Brave New World*, wrote that mind control has turned out to be not as blatant as Orwell predicted in *1984*, but rather more internalized and "fun":

> *...people will come to love their oppression, to adore the technologies that undo their capacities to think.*

So, turn off the television and the smartphone! Resist computer *click-bait*. Our media distracts us with barrages of innocuous fluff or endless repetitions of disasters in progress. Knowing how teachers have been unfairly demonized in the media should make us realize that the corporate-owned media also operates with a more serious agenda that both promotes its favored policies and demonizes those who stand in the way.

Liberating our minds thus requires us to find reliable sources of alternative news, analysis, and background information that challenge neoliberal capitalism wherever it seeks to exploit and oppress the vulnerable. For such sources of news and analysis, I suggest the following:

1. Progressive.org

The Progressive is a newsmagazine with insightful articles on domestic and international issues. It was founded during the Progressive Era by famed prairie progressive, Robert La Follette. (Neoliberal capitalists don't like to admit that Teddy Roosevelt was himself a progressive, the most famous one of that era.)

The Progressive is quite readable and a good introduction to progressive alternative media. It has a very relevant section on education called "Public School Shakedown."

2. Democracynow.org

Democracy Now produces TV programs that are available on the internet. Produced by highly skilled veteran reporters, it covers both domestic and international news from the perspective of the interests of the common people.

3. Telesurtv.net/English

Telesur is a joint television effort by South American countries that have thrown off the shackles imposed by neoliberalism. It focuses primarily on issues in the Americas but also covers other world issues and US domestic topics as well.

Read and watch the stories on this site to gain a coherent "Third World" perspective on world issues presented by reporters from the Global South. *Telesur* is also available in the original Spanish.

4. COUNTERPUNCH.ORG

Counterpunch lives up to its name! It is an incisive site that offers a different take on the same news items the corporate media presents. Indeed, it often exposes their subtle and gross distortions.

The contributors include many academics who provide excellent *background information* that the regular media neglects. This contextual information helps us to *understand the causes* of the instability in our world, whether it be the absurd hounding of teachers, the child refugees of Central America, Islamic fanaticism, or tribal warfare in Africa.

5. THENATION.COM

The Nation is the oldest weekly newsmagazine in the United States. It started as an abolitionist paper and is now the most respected voice of progressive news, analysis, and thought in America. Its website proudly boasts its distinguished contributors throughout history:

> *Henry James…Longfellow…W.E.B. Dubois, E.M. Forster, Emma Goldman, Sinclair Lewis, Willa Cather, H.L. Mencken, Upton Sinclair, Margaret Mead… Bertrand Russell, Pearl S. Buck, Albert Einstein, I.F. Stone, Eleanor Roosevelt, Hannah Arendt, Jean-Paul*

Sartre, ... Edmund Wilson, W.H. Auden... Martin Luther King, Jr., Gore Vidal, and Toni Morrison.

In fact, James Baldwin, Ralph Nader... published their first pieces in <u>The Nation</u>.

With such respected writers as those cited above, the articles on the listed sites will help us to better understand the problems that confront us. With our minds free, we can begin to create a world that is similarly free of the absurd injustices imposed by neoliberal capitalism.

By freeing our minds, learning from others, and being willing to act with our neighbors and co-workers, we can thus end the Kafka-esque nightmare that currently haunts not only American teachers but the entire world!

Conclusion:

Freedom through Fun!

DON'T JUST PUT this book aside. Act on it! Instead of passively watching television or playing with your smartphone, start a *Meetup* group called *The Teacher's Manifesto* to discuss what you have read with other members of your community.

Discuss the news and analyses in the magazines and websites I have suggested. Find other sources. Explore with your new friends how to make changes in your community and your world. Raise the issues you are reading about and working on with your family and old friends.

Invite some friends over to watch one of the great public-issues documentaries that are regularly produced. One example is *The Big Short*, a highly entertaining look at how Wall Street robbed us, caused the recession of 2008, and continues to create the conditions for future catastrophe. The film even mentions how teachers got the blame for the academic problems that the economic collapse caused for students!

Neoliberal capitalism thrives on us being separated from each other and tempts us with meaningless distractions that ensure such separation. It is only through regaining our human community and working together that we will be liberated from the absurd nightmares of an economic system that is destroying our schools, our working lives, our communities, our water, and our planet itself.

Have fun while you work for change! Just make sure that your *fun* doesn't leave too large a carbon footprint. Ensure that it brings you together with others instead of separating you from them. Most importantly, make sure that your fun brings out a better side of you rather than a worse side.

In the end, we will find that the most long-term, rewarding fun are the simple communal activities that our ancestors enjoyed while working together on the common problems they faced. In resurrecting their wisdom of <u>strength through community</u>, we will find our own deliverance.

Endnotes

Chapter 2: Salem Witches

i   Karen Armstrong, introduction to A Delusion of Satan: The Full Story of the Salem Witch Trials, by Frances Hill (Cambridge: Da Capo Press, 2002), ix.

Chapter 3: Barbarians on the Warpath!

ii   Phillip Harris, "Collateral Damage: The Problems of Teacher Assessment," *Rowmanblog*.typepad.com, October 8, 2010.

iii   *Idem.*

iv   *Idem.*

Chapter 4: Teachers as Witches

v   Karen Armstrong, introduction to *A Delusion of Satan: The Full Story of the Salem Witch Trials*, by Frances Hill (Cambridge: Da Capo Press, 2002), x.

vi   Pat Winger, "An Offer They Wouldn't Refuse," *Newsweek*, October 12, 2010.

vii   Tom LoBianco, "John Kasich Says If He Were 'King of America' He'd Ban Teachers' Lounges," *cnn*.com, October 19, 2015.

viii Ashley Burross, "Labor Settlement to have Far-Ranging Consequences," msechottopics.msec.org, November 17, 2011.

ix   Valerie Strauss, "Chris Christie Wants To Punch the Teachers Union in the Face. But He Is Not the Only Candidate Attacking Educators," *washingtonpost*.com, August 3, 2015.

Chapter 5: Scapegoating Betrays Hope

x   "The Lottery," www.*schmoop*.com

xi   "Los Angeles Teacher Ratings," *Los Angeles Times*, August 14, 2010.

xii   John Springer, "Obama: Money without Reform Won't Fix School System," *Today*.com, September 27, 2010.

Chapter 6: Destroying American Professionalism

xiii   Steve Bousquet, "Gov. Rick Scott Will Seek $1 B in Tax Cuts," *Miami Herald*, November 5, 2015.

xiv   Mark Twain, "The Lowest Animal."

Chapter 7: Bleeding the Patient Returns!

xv   Leonara L. Anton, et al., "Neglect, $100 Million in Cuts Create Chaos in State's Mental Hospitals," *Miami Herald*, November 1, 2015.

xvi   Ahiza Garcia, "Amazon's Culture Is 'Purposeful Darwinism' Investigation Finds," *money.cnn*.com, August 15, 2015.

xvii   Andre Spicer, "What Jeff Bezos Learned from Chairman Mao," *cnn*.com, August 18, 2015.

xviii   Robert Reich, "America Is a Nation of Amazons," *salon*.com, August 18, 2015.

xix   Emily Peck "Amazon Only Perfected what American Culture Created," *huffingtonpost*.com, August 17, 2015.

xx   John Newman, "The Grim Externalities of Amazon.com," *counterpunch*.org, August 17, 2015.

Chapter 8: Killing Kids

xxi   Carol Marbin Miller & Audra D.S. Burch, "Florida's Undercount of Child Abuse Deaths," *Miami Herald*, March 22, 2014.

xxii   Janie Campbell, "Rick Scott Blasted for Deaths of 40 Children," *huffingtonpost.com*, December 20, 2013.

xxiii   Amy Sherman, "Rick Scott 'Oversaw the Largest Medicare Fraud in the Nation's History,' Florida Democratic Party Says," *politifact*.com, March 3, 2014.

xxiv   Carol Marbin Miller, "Girl Recalls Horrors of Foster Care," *Miami Herald*, April 4, 2015.

xxv   Carol Marbin Miller, "State Strips Sick Kids of Healthcare, Doctors Say," *Miami Herald*, August 2, 2015.

xxvi   Carol Marbin Miller, "Mother: Violence at Lockup Cost Son His Life," *Miami Herald*, October 13, 2015.

xxvii   David Ovalle, "Foster Group under Fire over Video of Brawl," *Miami Herald*, January 13, 2016.

xxviii   Rebecca McCray, "Maryland Chooses Jail over Schools for Baltimore Youths," *takepart*.com, May 16, 2015.

xxix   *Idem.*

Chapter 9: The Death of Teacher Professionalism

xxx   Susan Edelman, "Principal Doesn't Want Teachers Sitting— So She Throws Out All Their Desks," *New York Post*, August 20, 2015.

Chapter 10: Two Privatization Warnings

xxxi   "The Failings of Chile's Education System: Institutionalized Inequality and a Preference for the Affluent," *Council on Hemispheric Affairs*, July 30, 2008.

xxxii   Michael Vasquez, "Owner of For-Profit College FastTrain Is Guilty of Theft," *Miami Herald*, November, 25, 2015.

xxxiii   Michael Vasquez, "Dade Medical College Owner Turns Himself In," *Miami Herald*, November 3, 2015.

xxxiv   *Idem.*

xxxv   *Idem.*

xxxvi   *Idem.*

xxxvii   Michael Vasquez, "Perez, Politicians: Friends to the End," *Miami Herald*, November 8, 2015.

xxxviii *Idem.*

xxxix   Michael Vasquez, "Higher-Ed Hustle," *Miami Herald*, Various dates, 2015.

xl   Karen Yi, "3 More Charters Facing Closure," *South Florida Sun Sentinel*, March 18, 2014.

xli   Jacob Carpenter, "Florida's Failed Charter Schools," *Naples Daily News*, September 20, 2014.

xlii   Scott Hiaasen and Kathleen McGrory. "Cashing In on Kids," *Miami Herald*, September 19, 2011.

xliii   Amy Shipley, "Charter Schools: Unsupervised," *South Florida Sun Sentinel*, June 18, 2014.

xliv   Michael Sallah et al., "A City, A Couple, A Scandal," *Miami Herald*, January 31, 2016.

xlv   Scott Travis, "School Board Member Withdraws Son from Public School," *South Florida Sun Sentinel*, September 30, 2013

Chapter 11: Why Teachers and Not Cops?

xlvi   Christopher Sherman, "FBI Director Blames Crime on Police Misconduct Videos," *huffingtonpost*.com, October 24, 2015.

xlvii   Elizabeth Koh, "Good Cop/Bad Cop," *Miami Herald*, November 22, 2015.

xlviii   Michael Sallah, "The Fall of Miami-Dade's Cash Cop," *Miami Herald*, October 4, 2015.

xlix   Fred Grimm, "Police Union Tactics Get Down, Dirty," *Miami Herald*, March 25, 2014.

l   "New Mexico Sheriff Convicted of Abuse during Traffic Stop," *cbsnews*.com, September 26, 2014.

li   Julie K. Brown, "In Miami Gardens, Store Video Catches Cops in the Act," *Miami Herald*, November 21, 2013.

lii   Julie K. Brown, "More Cops on Far Side of Law," *Miami Herald*, May 23, 2012.

liii   Julie K. Brown, "The Cop Who Won't Go Away," *Miami Herald*, July 1, 2012.

liv   Fred Grimm, "Firing Kid at Arby's Easier than Bad Cop," *Miami Herald*, September 6, 2015.

lv   Frances Robles, "Sanford Cops Lazy, Suspect Said in '11," *Miami Herald*, May 24, 2012.

lvi   Lisa J. Huriash, "Plantation Cop Suspended for Texting Abuse Victim," *South Florida Sun Sentinel*, August 5, 2011.

lvii   Julie K. Brown, and David Smiley, "Report: Lies, Negligence Led to Cop's ATV Crash," *Miami Herald*, October 2, 2011.

lviii   Frances Robles, "Puerto Rican Police Arrested in Drug Probe," *McClatchy Newspapers*, October 8, 2010.

lix   Geoff Mulvihill, "Terrorized Camden Residents Say Cops Worse Than Criminals," *Associated Press*, April 4, 2010. "Camden Police Allegedly Planted Evidence," *UPI*, October 15, 2010.

lx   John Holland, "FBI Agent Blasts Hollywood Police," *sun-sentinel*.com, October 16, 2008.

lxi   Tonya Alanez, "Ex-Hollywood Cop Accused of Doctoring Report Heads to Trial," *sun-sentinel*.com, November 27, 2011.

lxii   Steven Chermak Ph.D. and Frankie Y. Bailey, Ph.D., *Crimes of the Centuries: Notorious Crimes, Criminals, and Criminal Trials in American History*, (Kindle: ABC-CLIO, 2016), 531. "1980 Miami Riots," Wikipedia.org.

lxiii   Fred Grimm, "We Stopped Electing Sheriffs for a Reason," *Miami Herald*, December, 6, 2015.

lxiv   Charles Rabin, "In Miami, Murders Yield Fewer Results," *Miami Herald*, September 10, 2015.

lxv   Veronica Rocha, "Three Students Arrested after Fighting in the Florin High School Cafeteria Is Captured on Video," *latimes*.com, October 28, 2015.

lxvi   "Cafeteria Chaos at Miami Springs High Ends with Student's Arrest," *Miami Herald*, October 28, 2015.

About the Author

KRISHNA MADAN TEACHES History and English at a public high school in Florida. He is originally from the Caribbean, where teachers are treated quite differently. He has a Bachelor's Degree in International Affairs and two Master's Degrees: one in English Language and the other in Political Philosophy.

Krishna has taught from the elementary to the college level at private, parochial, and public schools. He even taught at the elitist prep school that Obama attended in Hawaii, giving him insight into Obama's and Gates' attitude to education.

Krishna is currently working on the sequel to *The Teacher's Manifesto*, but needs your help on this one. Please send him your stories about teaching, injustice, and any other topics in this book to *krish_m2k@hotmail.com*.

Join *The Teacher's Manifesto* on Facebook and follow Krishna on Twitter. Discuss the ideas in this book on social media.